One night a man came to our house and told me, "There is a family with eight children. They have not eaten for days," I took some food and I went. When I finally came to the family, I saw the faces of those little children disfigured by hunger. There was no sorrow or sadness in their faces, just the deep pain of hunger. I gave the rice to the mother. She divided it in two, and went out, carrying half the rice with her.

When she came back, I asked her, "Where did you go?" She gave me this simple answer, "To my neighbors – they are hungry also."

– Mother Teresa

Learning to Love Your Neighbor

Finding Your Place in God's Plan to Fix a Broken World

David L. Nichols

Learning to Love Your Neighbor: Finding Your Place in God's Plan to Fix a Broken World

ISBN-10: 1492831263   ISBN-13: 978-1492831266

Printed in the U.S.A.
CreateSpace
4900 LaCross Road
North Charleston, SC 29406

American Baptist
CHURCHES of MICHIGAN

4578 S. Hagadorn Rd.
E. Lansing, MI 48853

www.learningtoloveyourneighbor.com

Contents

FOREWORD

Then the Lord said to Cain, "Where is your brother Abel?" "I don't know," he replied. "Am I my brother's keeper?"

Genesis 4:9

I have been provoked and convicted by the writings of Bill Hull. In *The Complete Book of Discipleship: On Being and Making Followers of Christ*, he states, "Unfortunately non-discipleship Christianity dominates much of the thinking of the contemporary church...departing from the gospel that calls on all believers to be disciples and follow Christ in obedience."[1]

Since 1999 I have been privileged to serve as the Executive Minister of American Baptist Churches of Michigan. As I have served among our churches, I have become increasingly convinced we must dare to struggle, both individually and corporately, with this "non-discipleship Christianity" and in the struggle wrestle with these questions:

1. To whom do we really belong?
2. What is expected of us as followers of Christ—people of God?
3. What is it about our experience with Jesus that our community cannot live without?

Christians belong to Jesus Christ and to the community. We are called to grow more like Jesus; to share what Jesus has done in our lives with our brothers, sisters, friends, and neighbors. We are called to be counter-cultural, developing a community of care;

---

[1] Bill Hull, The Complete Book of Discipleship: On Being and Making Followers of Christ (Colorado Springs, CO: Navpress, 2006) page 41.

love; hope and trust in the midst of an anxious culture run amok. And yet, far too many individuals and congregations are turning inward and embracing "non-discipleship Christianity." I fear some churches risk becoming nothing more than poor men's country clubs where people go to have services rendered to them rather than equipped to go out into community sharing what Jesus has done in their lives. Churches run the danger of focusing upon remembering the story in and among themselves rather than being and sharing the story of Jesus beyond themselves in their communities.

If we are to be vibrant, vital communities of faith impacting our communities for the good, individually and corporately we must go deep in our relationship with Jesus. Individually and corporately we must discover what it is about our experience with Jesus, that is so unique, precious, and universally significant, that unless we share it with someone else, both of our lives will be lacking. In other words, out of our deepening relationship with Jesus we are compelled to do no less than reach out to neighbor for we are our sister, our brother, our neighbor's keeper!

Dr. Nichols invites all of us, individually and corporately, to grow in our love for God and in so doing move beyond "non-discipleship Christianity." In so doing all of us will be immeasurably enriched and the Kingdom of God expanded!

Rev. Dr. Michael L. Williams
Executive Minister
American Baptist Churches of Michigan

INTRODUCTION

"I am not sure exactly what heaven will be like, but I know that when we die and it comes time for God to judge us, he will not ask, 'How many good things have you done in your life?' rather he will ask, 'How much love did you put into what you did?"

— Mother Teresa

As part of our daily routine, my wife and I watch the evening news with Brian Williams on NBC. We think it's important to have an idea of what's happening around the world, though some days we aren't so sure. The effect of hearing about pain and suffering, greed and violence, one tragedy followed by another, day after day is sometimes more than we can bear. Love of God and love of neighbor are both woefully absent.

THE WORLD IS BROKEN

This may be hard to imagine, but a century ago, there were countless people who believed the world was getting better and better. Among other things, they believed science and education would bring the necessary enlightenment to solve all the world's problems.

Then came World War I, the Great Depression, World War II with the Holocaust and the atom bomb, and then the Cold War and its MAD policy of Mutually Assured Destruction. In a span of fifty years any talk of a better world had come to sound hopelessly idealistic.

Another fifty years have passed and the world strikes us as being so badly broken it can never be fixed. Occasionally there are signs of hope; even the NBC news ends with a "Making a Difference" segment that points out something good someone has done. However, most people today – and especially those who are younger – have a dim view of the world and its future.

The Bible says sin is at the heart of the world's problems. Sin is not a matter of breaking some arbitrary laws God has insisted we obey; it is putting ourselves first, seeking our own well-being at the expense of others. Sin is ultimately a love of self that leaves little room for either love of God or neighbor.

In one of life's great ironies, it is this love of self that inevitably becomes self-destructive. The end result is broken people living in a broken world. It looks like this:

- *A man enjoys the intimate embrace of a woman, but has no time for the child born as a result of it.*

- *A woman commits adultery and tells her husband of twenty years, "I never really loved you!"*

- *A company executive lays off older employees, demands more work at less pay from younger ones and is given a bonus for doing so.*

- *A leader kills tens of thousands of his own people in order to prop up his failing regime.*

- *A general sends troops into certain death in pursuit of a military objective of uncertain value.*

- *A group acts shamefully toward those of a different race, religion, ethnic origin or sexual orientation.*

These are but a few examples of human sinfulness and probably not even the worst. What they share in common, though, is the devastation and destruction they produce.

Unfortunately, our attempts to fix what's wrong with the world have accomplished little. We declared a war on drugs and imprisoned everyone who sold or possessed them, but what we ended up with 40 years and a trillion dollars later were over-crowded prisons and no appreciable decline in drug use. Many wonder what has been accomplished by "wars" on poverty, crime, or illegal immigration, or by our invasions of Iraq and Afghanistan.

GOD HAS A PLAN TO FIX OUR BROKEN WORLD

There isn't actually much new about the problems we face today. Our weapons may be more destructive than what has come before, but those who wield them are probably no more evil than our ancestors.

Some days we might wish we could eliminate everyone who is part of the problem. If we did so, however, there might not be anyone left.

The biblical story of Noah describes something like this. God wiped out the whole world and started all over with only one good man and his family. The flood didn't solve anything, though, because afterward God could see the inclination of the human heart to evil remained unchanged.

God's plan to fix a broken world began anew by calling Abraham, who was old and childless, to leave everything for a new land where he would be the founder of a new people. God entered into a covenant to be the Provider and Protector for Abraham and his countless descendants. Through Moses God gave his Law to let people know how they ought to live; God also prescribed a means of offering sacrifices when people failed to live as they should.

Some great things happened as the Chosen People lived in the Promised Land, but there were still huge problems. Rather than being a light to other nations, the Chosen People too often ended up being just like them. This national failure included a leadership problem as many of the kings lived in open rebellion against God.

Prophets arose to confront these evil rulers and to speak of God's plan for a coming king, an anointed Messiah, who would rule in righteousness, establishing a kingdom where the "shalom" (peace and well-being) God desired for the world would become a reality. People began to look forward to this "Day of the Lord" when the broken world would be fixed.

Hundreds of years passed and then Jesus burst on the scene saying, "The time has come; the kingdom of God is at hand. Turn from your evil ways and believe the good news." His proclamation of the coming kingdom was accompanied by acts of healing and other miraculous signs. God's light was shining in the darkness as the "shalom" of God began to impact our broken world.

Excited crowds followed Jesus in eager anticipation of what was to come if he truly was the Messiah, but no one was prepared for him to be arrested and crucified. Jesus had given hints of his sacrificial death all along, but everyone was too excited about his expected triumph to pay much attention to them.

The death of Jesus, however, was always central to God's plan because the harm people have done to one another was simply too great to overlook. God could simply have forgiven everyone who did wrong, but doing so would have trivialized every victim's pain and suffering in ways totally inconsistent with God's love.

Neither has it ever been possible for humanity to atone for the wrong they have done. A drunk driver who sobers up and convinces hundreds of others to act responsibly has still done nothing to make it right with the family whose child was killed in an alcohol-fueled accident. A bell once rung can never be unrung; a wrong once done can never be undone.

We all stand condemned for the hurtful things we ourselves have done and for the pain and suffering we have allowed to be done by others.

The price to be paid for all of this is beyond what any of us or all of us could pay even with our lives. The only suffering that could possibly atone for the suffering caused by humanity would be the suffering of God himself. This is the mystery and the miracle of the cross: Jesus, the Son of God who knew no sin, took the sins of humanity upon himself and died in our place.

The cross was at the heart of God's plan, but it was not the end of it. God raised Jesus from the dead, affirming the truth of everything Jesus had said and done. The resurrection also assured the return of Jesus as King of kings and Lord of lords, the promise of our own resurrection and life eternal in the recreated heavens and earth.

YOU HAVE A PLACE IN GOD'S PLAN

This is the story of God's plan to fix a broken world and you have a place in it. Simply believing the story, however, is not enough; God wants you to live it day by day.

God has not left us in the dark concerning how we ought to live. In Matthew 22:34-40 Jesus gave us a summary of everything God asks of us:

> *Hearing that Jesus had silenced the Sadducees, the Pharisees got together. One of them, an expert in the law, tested him with this question: "Teacher, which is the greatest commandment in the Law?"*
>
> *Jesus replied: "'Love the Lord your God with all your heart and with all your soul and with all your mind.' This is the*

first and greatest commandment. And the second is like it:
'Love your neighbor as yourself.' All the Law and the
Prophets hang on these two commandments.

By summarizing the Scriptures in this way, Jesus made it simple to obey God, but he did not make it easy.

To love God with all our heart, soul and mind calls for total commitment. It changes how we worship, what we value and how we live every aspect of our lives.

Likewise, to love our neighbor as ourselves sets the bar high. This is not about tolerating each other or learning to get along, but about caring as much about the well-being of others as we do about our own.

Neither love for God nor love for neighbor comes to us naturally; after all, we live in a world that teaches us the opposite. In order for us to love our neighbors (and even our enemies!) in the way God wants, there is much for us to learn and much for us to unlearn.

The purpose of this book is to help you grow in your love for God by learning to love your neighbor. As you experience this journey over the coming months, may you indeed find your place in God's plan to fix a broken world, and may the process of discovering it be the adventure of a lifetime!

BEFORE YOU BEGIN

Learning to love your neighbor has the potential to change your life, your church and your community as you find your place in God's plan to fix a broken world. There is little chance this will happen, though, unless you are willing to do certain things.

SPEND TIME WITH GOD

This book incorporates many passages of Scripture with which you may be familiar if you have grown up in church. Let them become new and fresh as you immerse yourself in them in order for God to speak to you through them. This happens best in a dedicated "quiet time" each day, but it could be time spent commuting, exercising, eating or some other activity that lets you focus on God; in other words, multi-tasking is *not* helpful here.

You will benefit from reading the material early in the week and then reflecting on it throughout the week, reading the Scriptures and questions over again as necessary. Note what stands out to you in the Scripture passage and what reflection question strikes a nerve. This is often how God speaks to you; be open to what God is trying to say.

CONNECT WITH OTHERS

Most of us need to make a paradigm shift from thinking of ourselves as individuals to thinking of ourselves as part of a community. Going through this book with others will allow you to have shared insights and experiences that are priceless. This can be done in a variety of formats:

In a Large Group: you may be part of a Sunday School class or other group that would like to go through "Learning to Love Your Neighbor." My only caution is that you allow opportunity for everyone to talk. If your group has more than 6-8 people in it, some will rarely speak. Your group might want to consider breaking into smaller groups for part of the time and then coming back for the final 15 minutes in which a spokesperson for each group could share a few highlights.

In a Small Group: you may already be part of a small group that would like to go through this book together. Be sure the group recognizes some things in "Learning to Love Your Neighbor" might be different from what the group has normally done. In particular, involvement in ministry is a key element as explained below. If your group is ready for this new direction, go for it!

With a Partner: if you are not part of a large or small group, invite one or two (or more) friends to read through this book with you. Just be sure you connect with each other regularly to talk about what God is doing in your life.

For assistance with a small group, see the back of this book or visit our www.learningtoloveyourneighbor.com website.

Engage in Ministry

Reflection and discussion are important, but if you stop there you will miss the most important part. In Matthew 7:24-27 Jesus says only those who put into practice what he says are building on a rock-solid foundation; those who don't might as well be building on shifting sand.

You cannot learn to love your neighbor unless you put into practice what you learn. This can be done within the ministry contexts you already have:

- Where you work or live
- Where you or your children go to school
- A club or social group where you are involved
- Your family and friends

You may not think of the above as ministry contexts, but any place that has people in need provides opportunity for love in action.

Your ministry context can also be someplace entirely new to you. The time will come when you will be asked (and feel led) to go outside your comfort zone to serve someone with whom you have no previous connection and think you have nothing in common. This context of ministry might be:

- A food pantry or soup kitchen
- A homeless shelter
- A nursing home or senior citizen center
- Any place where there are people in need

Not everyone in your group has to be involved in the same ministry context, but doing so will give you a shared experience.

◇ ◇ ◇ ◇ ◇ ◇

What can you expect if you spend time with God, connect with others and engage in ministry as suggested here? Everyone's experience will be unique, but there are likely to be some common themes shared by all.

YOU WILL HEAR FROM GOD

You may find the question, "What has God been saying to you lately?" to be daunting, awkward or even weird. Do some people actually hear God's voice boom from the sky as in Bill Cosby's classic "Noah" comedy routine?

God may have "thundered" to Noah like he did when giving the Law to Moses on Mt. Sinai, but more typically the Bible speaks of God's "still, small voice." The whispers of God can easily be drowned out by other voices clamoring for our attention. This is why we encourage you to spend quiet time with God.

Sometimes God speaks to us in times of prayer and reflection. This rarely happens, of course, if our reflection time is filled with everything we want to tell God. Have a time of silence in your reflection and let God whisper to you.

Sometimes God speaks to us through people. Those who have a close relationship with God may feel led to tell us something God has placed on their heart. They can also be extremely helpful in discerning whether an idea we think has come to us from God really has.

Sometimes God speaks to us through experiences. Seeing a sunset, smelling a flower, touching a baby, hearing a song, feeding someone who is homeless: all these and many other experiences can be occasions to hear the quiet voice and sense the awesome presence of God.

Most often God speaks to us through Scripture. The Spirit who inspired those who wrote the Bible is the same Spirit who speaks to those who read it. Countless times I have been amazed by seeing something new in a passage I had previously read (and even preached!) on many occasions. This is God's Spirit at work. I know you'll experience this same activity of the Spirit as you immerse yourself in Scripture and spend time with God.

GOD WILL BRING PEOPLE INTO YOUR LIFE

As you begin to look at people differently and listen to their stories, as you serve these individuals and share with them some part of God's story, you will find yourself connecting to people in new ways.

As a pilot project for this book, I did a "90-Day 'Love Your Neighbor' Adventure" at Harbert Community Church where I was serving as Interim Pastor. Two people came into my life during that experience in unexpected ways.

The first was at the Secretary of State's office as I waited to have the address on my driver's license changed. I was not pleased to hear there would be a 90-minute wait, but I found a chair in the busy lobby. After a few minutes, the young man next to me leaned over and asked quietly, "Are you a pastor?"

I was shocked at his question and asked whatever made him think I might be. He said he really didn't know, and went on to ask many questions. He spoke at some length about why he was questioning his faith and no longer attending the church in which he had been raised. I mainly listened to him, and let him know God was not shocked by his doubts and questions.

A few weeks later, God brought another person into my life in a remarkable way. When she called the church and asked for help, I invited her to come by and tell me her story.

Having a homeless person come to the church and ask for help had happened several times in the previous months, but this woman was different. I found myself deeply touched by her story, particularly when she told me she and her fiancé hoped to find a church where he would not be judged for his extensive tattoos.

I was struck by the fact I had recently preached about not judging people on outward appearances. When the woman came into my office, I was working on a Bible study based on what Jesus said in Matthew 25:38, "I was a stranger and you took me in." All of this felt like it was way more than a coincidence.

YOU WILL HAVE LIFE-CHANGING EXPERIENCES

The outcome of these two unexpected encounters had only one thing in common: both profoundly impacted my life. I haven't seen the young man from the Secretary of State's office since that day, but the incredible way he came into my life left a lasting impression on me.

I have stayed in touch with the homeless woman and her tattooed fiancé. In fact, my wife and I invited them and their three children to live with us while they saved up for a place of their own, and our church gave them quite a wedding! I feel profoundly blessed to have this family in our life.

I don't know how God will touch your life over these next six months, but I am convinced your commitment to God and your openness to God's presence and power will result in something profound. This is the kind of thing that happens when you find your place in God's plan to fix a broken world.

www.learningtoloveyourneighbor.com

STEP ONE: ACCEPTING

Learning to Love Your Neighbor starts with following Jesus because, well, that's where it all starts. 1 John 4:19 puts it this way: "We love because he first loved us."

All of us are on a spiritual journey, with each of us moving at a different pace, and some hardly moving at all. My own journey certainly has had plenty of starts and stops.

I grew up on a Wisconsin dairy farm in a community that had a Baptist church known for its commitment to mission. The church had been started in the 1840s and when I was there it had grown to about 200 members; I was related to more than 100 of them.

My family attended church regularly and I learned about Jesus at an early age in Sunday School and Vacation Bible School. When I was in 5th grade, a stern and rather scary teacher told our class if we didn't accept Jesus as our Savior we would go to hell when we died and would suffer there forever. That was enough for me to raise my hand and say I would accept Jesus.

I continued to be involved in church throughout grade school and then somewhat sporadically in high school after my family moved to Missouri. I spent a lot of time in a small Southern Baptist church while I was dating the pastor's daughter.

Early in my freshman year in college, a staff member from Campus Crusade for Christ knocked on my door and changed my life. He left my room encouraged from meeting his first Christian on campus, a conclusion he reached because I knew the Bible verses he shared with me.

My reaction to him was just the opposite: I wondered whether I was a Christian at all. His faith struck me as personal and vital; by comparison, mine was impersonal and empty. I wasn't sure I understood the exact nature of his relationship with God, but I knew it was what I wanted.

He invited me to be part of a Leadership Training Group and I felt quite honored. Later I discovered everyone gets asked to be part of such a group. In any case, I became very active and by the next year was leading the Campus Crusade group.

In the middle of my sophomore year, everything fell apart for me. All the Crusade staff members left town for a few weeks and I began to realize most of my faith was dependent on their presence. I still had no real connection with God, but what I did have was a lot of questions. Crusade staff had encouraged me not to worry because God would answer them in time. Unfortunately, my doubts erupted and I came to the unfortunate conclusion that Christian faith was only for the naïve who asked no questions. Thus began a period of reluctant atheism for me; I wanted to believe in God, but concluded to do so was intellectually untenable.

In the middle of my junior year in college, I had another unexpected encounter that was also life-changing as I spent time with a young woman from a Pentecostal church. As she told me the story of her life, I couldn't help but notice how it fit in with what I had been studying in my Sociology of Religion class. There was, however, a big difference between reading an abstract, academic description and hearing a vivid, personal testimony. I kept wondering which was true: the professor's explanations or the woman's experience. Was it even possible both could be true?

This encounter set me off on a new chapter in my spiritual journey. I began reading everything I could find by C. S. Lewis,

Francis Schaeffer, Elton Trueblood and a host of others who dealt with the intellectual questions that plagued me.

Over a period of months, I began to sense a major change taking place in my life as doubt gave way to faith. Something was happening to me intellectually, but even more was happening to me at a profoundly personal level as I encountered Jesus in ways I had never imagined.

Much has happened in the years since that first encounter and I have heard God's call many times and in many ways. To tell about each of these steps in my journey would take too much time for the purposes of this book.

What is more important right now is **your** spiritual journey. It is my hope and prayer you will in the coming weeks hear God's call in new ways as you reflect on some of the Scriptures that have impacted me so powerfully. If you do encounter Jesus in this way, your life will never be the same.

1.1 ACCEPTING THE MISSION

In college I discovered Hal Lindsay's "Late Great Planet Earth" and quickly became obsessed with biblical end-times prophecies. Before long I was trying to learn all I could about the Rapture, the Mark of the Beast, the Antichrist and a host of other things from Daniel, Ezekiel and Revelation.

What a waste of time! Not only did I eventually figure out that most of the "scholars" who wrote about prophecy were more than a little goofy, but I realized focusing on **when** everything would happen was causing me to lose focus on **what** was going to happen and **how** God was calling me to live in the meantime.

I don't want to be like those who have given up on the world and are just waiting for Jesus to come and take them to heaven. This abandonment of earth is definitely not what the Bible teaches. Both the Old and New Testaments speak of a day when a renewed creation will experience the "shalom" (peace and well-being) God intended from the beginning.

REVELATION 21:1-4

Then I saw "a new heaven and a new earth," for the first heaven and the first earth had passed away, and there was no longer any sea. I saw the Holy City, the new Jerusalem, coming down out of heaven from God, prepared as a bride beautifully dressed for her husband. And I heard a loud voice from the throne saying, "Look! God's dwelling place is now among the people, and he will dwell with them. They will be his people, and God himself will be with them and be their

God. *'He will wipe every tear from their eyes. There will be no more death' or mourning or crying or pain, for the old order of things has passed away."*

Jesus will return one day as the King of kings, and the kingdom of heaven will come to a new and restored earth in the culmination of all history. On that day, we will be given our resurrected bodies and there will be no more tears, no more suffering and no more death.

In the meantime, as we wait for God's kingdom to come in its fullness, we celebrate the way God dwells among us even now. In great and small ways, God's kingdom is breaking in already.

> *How do you view the world today? In what ways are things getting worse or better? Apart from the return of Jesus, do you look to the future more with hope or despair?*

MARK 1:14-15

After John was put in prison, Jesus went into Galilee, proclaiming the good news of God. "The time has come," he said. "The kingdom of God has come near. Repent and believe the good news!"

Jesus believed the kingdom of God was not a distant future hope, but something whose time had come. The nearness of God's kingdom was the central message of John the Baptist, Jesus and the early disciples. Those who heard this message assumed it meant the imminent defeat of Rome, Satan and all God's enemies. When they saw God's power demonstrated in the miracles of Jesus, they thought the day they had longed for was at hand.

Unfortunately, almost everyone missed the "already but not yet" character of God's kingdom: it was already breaking into the world, but would not come in its fullness just yet.

In the meantime, people were to pray for the kingdom as Jesus taught: "Thy kingdom come, thy will be done on earth as it is in heaven." They were also to work for God's kingdom, allowing shalom (peace and well-being) to break into our world wherever there is suffering and need.

God's kingdom comes in large and small ways as people repent and believe. It is unfortunate these two terms are often understood so differently today than in their biblical context.

Repenting is not about feeling sorry for our sins, but about changing the direction of our lives. It means seeing things in a new light, viewing life from the perspective of God's kingdom rather than looking at things the way everyone in the world does.

Believing is not about agreeing with certain statements, but about acting in accordance with them. Seeing life in new ways from a kingdom of God perspective means little if we don't live our lives consistent with that perspective.

> *How do you respond to this biblical definition of what it means to repent and believe? Is your life on track and headed in a good direction? What do you find hardest about living your faith?*

LUKE 19:41-44

As he approached Jerusalem and saw the city, he wept over it and said, "If you, even you, had only known on this day what would bring you peace—but now it is hidden from your eyes. The days will come upon you when your enemies will build an embankment against you and encircle you and hem you in on every side. They will dash you to the ground, you and the children within your walls. They will not leave one stone on another, because you did not recognize the time of God's coming to you."

Jesus wept for those who failed to grasp the hope of God's kingdom. He saw the leaders of his own people in Jerusalem choosing to pursue paths of death and destruction rather than seeking God's kingdom by repenting and believing.

About thirty years after the death of Jesus, Jerusalem was indeed destroyed by the Romans in response to Jewish rebellion and uprising.

> *Where in today's world do you see people choosing paths that lead to death and destruction?*

FOR REFLECTION AND DISCUSSION

To the extent you are comfortable doing so, share with your group your responses to the above questions and the following:

How would you explain what God's mission is for us today?
In what way has your life been impacted by that mission?

PRAYER

Let my heart be broken, Lord, for the things that break your heart. Help me know how I might be a voice for peace in a world of shrill voices raised in anger. Give me glimpses of your kingdom day by day as I follow where you lead.

1.2 Accepting the Call

When I told my father I wanted to go to seminary after college, he wasn't very happy about it at first. He was convinced a life of ministry meant a life of poverty and he wanted to spare me that. In time he came to appreciate the joy and fulfillment I found in ministry, and was proud of the difference I was making in people's lives.

I've always envied people who had a clear calling. My own call was not to a particular career, but to go wherever God led and do whatever God said. I've always felt I was right where God wanted me to be, and yet never have had a sense that I knew what I'd be doing five years in the future.

Those who follow Jesus do not all travel the same path. We come from different places, have different backgrounds and different interests. We hear the call of Jesus in unique ways. Some are well-prepared by what they have already learned in church or through life experiences; others are clueless about what awaits them.

Matthew 4:18-22

As Jesus was walking beside the Sea of Galilee, he saw two brothers, Simon called Peter and his brother Andrew. They were casting a net into the lake, for they were fishermen. "Come, follow me," Jesus said, "and I will send you out to fish for people." At once they left their nets and followed him.

Going on from there, he saw two other brothers, James son of Zebedee and his brother John. They were in a boat with their father Zebedee, preparing their nets. Jesus called them, and immediately they left the boat and their father and followed him.

Simon Peter, Andrew, James and John were not spending a leisurely day at the lake fishing: this was their business, their livelihood.

Jesus saw a connection between what they had been doing and what they could be doing in the future. He called them to refocus their skills and abilities toward a new cause: fishing for people.

> *Nothing is ever wasted in God's economy. What skills and insights have you gained in one context that God later used in another?*

LUKE 5:27-32

After this, Jesus went out and saw a tax collector by the name of Levi sitting at his tax booth. "Follow me," Jesus said to him, and Levi got up, left everything and followed him.

Then Levi held a great banquet for Jesus at his house, and a large crowd of tax collectors and others were eating with them. But the Pharisees and the teachers of the law who belonged to their sect complained to his disciples, "Why do you eat and drink with tax collectors and sinners?"

Jesus answered them, "It is not the healthy who need a doctor, but the sick. I have not come to call the righteous, but sinners to repentance."

There were many people who saw the tax collector that day, but probably no one other than Jesus saw him as a potential disciple. Tax collectors were despised and hated for being corrupt and for collecting taxes on behalf of Rome.

It is likely nothing in Levi's life prepared him to follow Jesus. When he "got up, left everything and followed," he was literally leaving his old life behind and moving into totally uncharted territory.

Levi may not have had any idea where his journey with Jesus would take him, but this apparently didn't trouble him at all. His joy in being given the opportunity to follow Jesus was so great he invited people to his home for a party.

Do you connect in any way with the calling of the tax collector? In what way does following Jesus involve a major break for you from who you have been and what you have done?

How likely would you be to throw a party to let people know God had done something wonderful in your life?

FOR REFLECTION AND DISCUSSION

To the extent you are comfortable doing so, share with your group the answers to the above questions and the following one:

In what way has your life been impacted by a call to follow Jesus and be involved in God's mission?

PRAYER

Help me, Lord, to hear your call ever more clearly and to be ready to follow wherever you lead me.

1.3 ACCEPTING THE GIFT

Years ago I preached a sermon that included the story of Jane Fonda's spiritual journey from atheism to faith. After the service a member of the congregation came up to me and he was obviously disturbed.

"Jane Fonda was a traitor to our country during the Vietnam War. She could never be a Christian!" the man thundered.

I was shocked at the depth of his anger for something that had happened more than thirty years before; I was also shocked at his inability to comprehend grace.

Many people have a functional understanding of grace almost the opposite of what it actually is. Grace is always the gift of God's unconditional love; it is never something that we can earn, merit or deserve.

Jesus proclaimed life in God's kingdom as a gift available to all, not the entitlement of a privileged few. What he said about entering the kingdom delighted some and disturbed others.

Jesus knew the shalom (peace and well-being) of God's kingdom would not come to Israel by rebellion against Rome. In his teaching and by his example, he presented a dramatically new understanding of what God's kingdom was, how it would come and who would be in it.

MARK 10:13-16

People were bringing little children to Jesus for him to place his hands on them, but the disciples rebuked them. When

Jesus saw this, he was indignant. He said to them, "Let the little children come to me, and do not hinder them, for the kingdom of God belongs to such as these. Truly I tell you, anyone who will not receive the kingdom of God like a little child will never enter it." And he took the children in his arms, placed his hands on them and blessed them.

In today's world, where children are so often the focus of attention, it is hard to imagine there was a time when women and children counted for little.

The disciples were at the point where they had begun to realize Jesus was the promised Messiah. As such, he was far too important to be bothered by children.

Jesus not only failed to share the disciples' perspective, he was indignant with them for their failure to grasp his message. A child's humility, simple faith, dependence and sense of awe were exactly what was needed for anyone wishing to enter God's kingdom.

> *How would you explain the difference between being childish and being childlike? Which positive characteristics of a child are the hardest for you to emulate?*

MARK 10:21-25

Jesus looked at him and loved him. "One thing you lack," he said. "Go, sell everything you have and give to the poor, and you will have treasure in heaven. Then come, follow me."

At this the man's face fell. He went away sad, because he had great wealth.

Jesus looked around and said to his disciples, "How hard it is for the rich to enter the kingdom of God!"

The disciples were amazed at his words. But Jesus said again, "Children, how hard it is to enter the kingdom of God! It is easier for a camel to go through the eye of a needle than for someone who is rich to enter the kingdom of God."

Jesus loved the man in this story and spoke to him not out of anger, but out of deep concern. Jesus could see the man's wealth was not bringing him the good life as he imagined, but actually keeping him from it.

Such an attitude was as preposterous to the disciples as the idea of a camel going through a needle's eye. They believed, along with everyone else in their world, that wealth was a blessing from God and poverty a curse. Surely, they thought, those who were blessed with wealth would be the first to enter the kingdom.

Jesus taught that the advantages of wealth in this world were disadvantages when it came to God's kingdom. How does your understanding of wealth relate to what Jesus taught here? If this rich man had the wrong attitude toward wealth, what would a right attitude look like?

JOHN 1:9-13

The true light that gives light to everyone was coming into the world. He was in the world, and though the world was made through him, the world did not recognize him. He came to his own land, but his own people did not receive him. Yet to all who did receive him, to those who believed in his name, he gave the right to become children of God— children born not of natural descent, nor of human decision or a husband's will, but born of God.

The Gospel of John's Christmas story has no angels, no shepherds, and no wise men; it doesn't even have Mary and Joseph. The only thing it has is the eternal Word, the light of life, becoming human and entering into a world of darkness. That is enough.

Receiving Jesus means welcoming him into your life and acknowledging him as the Son of God, the true Light that once came (and still comes) to a world of darkness.

> *Those who welcomed Jesus were given the right to become God's children. What has becoming God's child looked like in your life? Was it something that happened all at once or over a period of time?*

FOR REFLECTION AND DISCUSSION

To the extent you are comfortable doing so, share with your group your responses to the above questions and to the following one:

What obstacles to living as God's child with childlike faith have you encountered?

PRAYER

Help me never take for granted, Lord, the miracle of being your beloved child! Let nothing keep me from living with childlike faith in your love and protection.

1.4 Accepting the Example

At the end of 2009, the First Baptist Church of Royal Oak where I was pastor entered into merger talks with Genesis, a young and vibrant church in the same town. The merger faced many obstacles, two of which involved me directly: I would need to step down as pastor and I would need to stay in the church and let Beau McCarthy, the pastor of Genesis, become my pastor.

The first problem was solved rather easily because I was already thinking of taking early retirement in order to work with a number of churches on issues of stewardship and discipleship. Accepting such a position would make it possible for me to stay at Genesis throughout the early years of transition.

The second problem was also solved more easily than I had imagined. Beau told me Genesis had grown from 100 to 400 in less than ten years, and yet he and others felt all was not well because the growth in numbers had not been accompanied by growth in discipleship. His calling became very clear at that point: it was not about pastoring a church; it was about making disciples. He also told me he knew he had much to learn about being a disciple before he could hope to make disciples of others.

It didn't take long to figure out it would be a privilege to have Beau as my pastor.

It is wonderful to be given new life as God's child, but no one who follows Jesus can coast from that point forward. The way Jesus lived challenges everything we've been taught about how we should live.

LUKE 9:57-58

As they were walking along the road, a man said to him, "I will follow you wherever you go."

Jesus replied, "Foxes have dens and birds have nests, but the Son of Man has no place to lay his head."

Jesus didn't own anything except the clothes on his back. He was homeless, dependent completely on the generosity of others for his support.

This was the life Jesus chose at thirty years of age. Up to that point, we know he lived as the son of a carpenter, and most likely took up the trade himself.

When Jesus began his ministry, he chose a life dependent on God for everything he needed. He was not promoting some abstract ideal when he told the disciples to pray, "Give us this day our daily bread."

Within our culture, it is easy to allow the things we have to define who we are. What would you miss most if you lost everything? Would you feel like you were less of a person if you were homeless and penniless?

JOHN 13:12-17

When he had finished washing their feet, he put on his clothes and returned to his place. "Do you understand what I have done for you?" he asked them. "You call me 'Teacher' and 'Lord,' and rightly so, for that is what I am. Now that I, your Lord and Teacher, have washed your feet, you also should wash one another's feet. I have set you an example that you should do as I have done for you. Very truly I tell you, no servant is greater than his master, nor is a messenger greater than the one who sent him. Now that you know these things, you will be blessed if you do them.

Jesus and the disciples walked everywhere they went in a dry and dusty land that had neither sidewalks nor paved roads; by the end of the day, it was impossible not to be dirty.

Washing a guest's feet was a sign of hospitality. It was not the host who would do this, but the lowliest of servants.

> By washing the disciples' feet, Jesus showed no act of service was beneath his dignity. What lowly acts of service might you find particularly challenging or even disgusting?

LUKE 23:32-34

Two other men, both criminals, were also led out with him to be executed. When they came to the place called the Skull, they crucified him there, along with the criminals—one on his right, the other on his left. Jesus said, "Father, forgive them, for they do not know what they are doing." And they divided up his clothes by casting lots.

When Jesus said we should love our enemies, he was not being an idealist with no idea how things were in "the real world." Jesus lived what he taught.

Those who crucified Jesus were more interested in his clothes than his life, and yet he asked God to forgive the enormity of their sin. He could not have done this without seeing something in them worth forgiving. Even those who crucified Jesus had been created in the image of God.

It is hard to imagine any act of love more extreme than what Jesus did on the cross. He died not only for those who followed him, but even for those who treated him so cruelly.

Think of someone who has hurt you or threatened a loved one. Do you feel justified in hating this person? Do you think it would be possible for you to ever forgive what was done?

For Reflection and Discussion

To the extent you are comfortable doing so, share with your group your responses to the above questions and the following one:

What about the way Jesus lived challenges you most deeply?

Prayer

Help me find meaning and purpose, Lord, in humble acts of service. As I marvel at the undeserved love you have for me, give me the grace and courage to love others who are also undeserving.

MINISTRY REFLECTIONS

As you complete the first section of *Learning to Love Your Neighbor*, it would be good for you to reflect on the following questions:

1. ***Are you finding time for God?*** *It is true there is no set amount of time required, but it is also true if you are not able to find time to read the Scriptures and reflect on them, not much will happen.*

2. ***Are you joining with others?*** *It doesn't matter a lot whether you are reading this book with a partner, a small group or an entire church. Reading it by yourself, however, will severely limit what you can learn and experience.*

3. ***Have you found a place for ministry?*** *This can be any group of people dealing with life's issues as long as you have freedom to engage with them. Until you find where God can use you, though, this book will never be anything more than interesting ideas.*

If you answered "No" to any of these questions, the good news is it isn't too late to do something about it. Before going further in this book, be sure these three critical elements are in place.

STEP TWO: SEEING

When I was a child, I used to go with my uncle and cousin to the County Fairgrounds to watch professional wrestling. After the show, I would collect as many autographs as I could.

As I look back on it now, I wonder why I thought these wrestlers were so special. They were big and strong, of course, but there wasn't much else about them particularly admirable or noteworthy. They were celebrities, though, and I thought that made them important.

Celebrity worship is part of American culture. Magazines detail the latest gossip about the rich and famous. News accounts relate the decisions of those in power, most of whom got where they are more by wealth and connections than by ability and hard work. For some reason, though, these are the people we imagine to be on top of the world and we treat them accordingly.

The people we imagine to be on the bottom are treated just the opposite. America imprisons more people than any other country because we would rather lock away "trouble-makers" than seek to help them. Likewise, we do everything we can to see those who are poor stay in ghettoes where we think they belong and not disturb those who live in nice communities. Everybody thinks there should be more places and organizations that help people in need as long as they are NIMBY (not in my back yard).

Such attitudes are typical in our culture, and they stand in stark contrast to the values of God's kingdom. One of the biggest changes that comes into our lives when we follow Jesus is seeing people from an entirely different perspective.

Those we think are at the top rarely are. This is a lesson I first learned as an undergraduate at Harvard. Until then, when I looked at people who were rich and famous, I assumed they had it all. As I got to know some of them, however, I began to see their lives were no more problem-free than anyone else's.

- *I saw children of privilege who drove expensive cars and vacationed around the world, but who longed for gifts of affection and attention their parents couldn't buy and wouldn't give.*

- *I saw people who were highly intelligent, but whose life choices revealed little if any wisdom. In the classroom they showed ability to grasp complex issues and solve intricate problems, but in life they seemed clueless about how to find a life of meaning and fulfilment.*

- *I saw a Miss America whose beauty was matched only by her insecurity. Others saw her as incredibly attractive, but she could only see what she thought were flaws in her appearance.*

In each of these cases I came to see how people could from one perspective have everything, but from another perspective have nothing. I also came to see how the opposite could be true.

Those we think are at the bottom rarely are. I learned this lesson repeatedly in a lifetime of ministry, with some of the most powerful examples coming on mission trips. Every time I saw people living in dire circumstances, I also saw more peace and joy than I would ever have expected.

As we follow Jesus, there is a lot we need to learn and maybe even more we need to unlearn. It all begins with seeing people in new ways.

2.1 Seeing Flaws

I once read that 90% of people think they are "above average" drivers. This may be one of those statistics my wife is always accusing me of pulling out of thin air, but it sounds about right when I consider how many bad drivers are out there.

Other drivers bring out the worst in people. We become annoyed when someone passes us and then slows down to the point we have to pass them. We get upset when someone drives right on our bumper. We get angry when people fail to use turn signals. We go ballistic when someone cuts in front of us. Or at least I do.

The number of things in our world able to upset us is almost endless, and every one of them involves some level of judgment and condemnation on our part. Being angry at everything and everybody isn't hard; showing grace and trying to understand why people act the way they do is a huge challenge.

Because we live in a broken world, it is easy to see how everyone is part of the problem, or more accurately how everyone *else* is part of the problem.

This kind of thinking is all too common. When it comes to self-evaluation, we compare ourselves to someone worse than we think we are. We usually don't have to look far to find someone who fits the description.

The world Jesus lived in had the same problem.

JOHN 8:4-9

"Teacher, this woman was caught in the act of adultery. Moses commanded us to stone such women. What do you say?" They were using this question as a trap, in order to have a basis for accusing him.

Jesus bent down and started to write on the ground with his finger. When they kept on questioning him, he straightened up and said to them, "Let any one of you who is without sin be the first to throw a stone at her." Again he stooped and wrote on the ground.

At this, those who heard began to go away one at a time, the older ones first, until only Jesus was left with the woman still standing there.

If this woman was caught "in the act of adultery," what happened to the man? According to the Law of Moses both were subject to the same death penalty.

What the Pharisees really wanted was to trap Jesus: if he said this woman should be stoned, he would be going against Roman law; if he said she should not be stoned, he would be going against Jewish Law.

It was Jesus, of course, they really wanted to stone. In their own eyes, this was simply an "innocent" way to attack him. Any answer Jesus gave would get him in trouble.

Jesus first refused to answer their question; writing on the ground was a way of dismissing them. When they persisted, he gave an answer that put them to shame as they were forced to look more closely at themselves.

Throwing stones is barbaric; our own world has perfected far more civilized means of destroying people. Political campaigns in recent years have become increasingly ugly as candidates and their friends have spent enormous amounts of money and shaded the truth until it was indistinguishable from outrageous lies in order to damage their opponent.

> *Besides political dirty tricks, what other ways have we found to destroy people we don't like? Who today is most likely to bear the brunt of such attacks?*

MATTHEW 7:1-5

Do not judge, or you too will be judged. For in the same way you judge others, you will be judged, and with the measure you use, it will be measured to you.

Why do you look at the speck of sawdust in your brother's eye and pay no attention to the plank in your own eye? How can you say to your brother, "Let me take the speck out of your eye," when all the time there is a plank in your own eye? You hypocrite, first take the plank out of your own eye, and then you will see clearly to remove the speck from your brother's eye.

Jesus is showing little subtlety here in confronting our tendency to be judgmental. He reminds us how ridiculous it is to imagine we can see other people's problems with crystal clarity while remaining blissfully unaware of our own.

> *We are all critical and judgmental at times. What do you most criticize about others? What problems are you most likely to ignore in your own life? What would need to change in your life in order to offer more grace to others?*

FOR REFLECTION AND DISCUSSION

To the extent you are comfortable doing so, share with your group your responses to the above questions and the following:

Many of us are deeply judgmental toward those we perceive as being bigoted, intolerant and close-minded. How might we avoid being judgmental toward those we think are judgmental?

PRAYER

Humble me, Lord, when I lose sight of my own need for grace in my haste to throw stones at others. Give me courage to stand up for those who are bullied or abused.

2.2 Seeing Hearts

Sometimes experience makes us confront the prejudice we would prefer to pretend we don't have. Years ago I was driving through a not so nice part of Gary, Indiana on my way to speak at a church. When I realized I had a flat tire, I began to worry about what might happen next.

As I started to change the flat, I was approached by a very large African-American I would have described as "looking like a thug." No one else was around and I felt very vulnerable. As he approached, he asked where I was going and I told him I was on my way to church. He said, "Why don't you let me change that tire for you so you don't get those nice church clothes dirty."

I was still suspicious of him, but after he finished changing the tire, I thanked him and tried to pay him. He said it was just his good deed for the day; all he asked was that I say a prayer in church for him and help the next person I found in trouble.

Needless to say, this was not at all what I expected! My first reaction was to think it was an answered prayer. Then I realized what it really was: a rather painful reminder of how I was seeing people through eyes of prejudice.

There is an old adage that says, "You never get a second chance to make a first impression." There is a truth in this and yet it is unfortunate because outward appearance – whether positive or negative – is rarely a true reflection of who a person is. Even an Old Testament prophet like Samuel was mistaken when it came to knowing who had the makings of a king.

1 SAMUEL 16:6-7

When they arrived, Samuel saw Eliab and thought, "Surely the Lord's anointed stands here before the Lord."

But the Lord said to Samuel, "Do not consider his appearance or his height, for I have rejected him. The Lord does not look at the things people look at. People look at the outward appearance, but the Lord looks at the heart."

Samuel, conditioned by culture to see the oldest son as the leader of the family's next generation, saw at a glance what an impressive man Jesse's oldest son was. Contrary to all cultural standards, however, God told Samuel to anoint Jesse's youngest son, David, to be the new king. It turned out to be a great choice.

This was not an isolated example; Isaac, Jacob, Joseph, Moses and a host of others were younger sons who didn't look much like leaders when God chose them.

Our world today still has difficulty seeing people for who they are and what they might become. Dustin Hoffman insisted a make-up artist make him look like "a real woman" for his role in "Tootsie." When viewing the results, he commented he indeed looked like a woman, but what he really wanted was to be beautiful. The artist told him it couldn't be done.

This encounter led to a painful epiphany for the actor as he realized how long he had lived with the assumption only beautiful women were truly interesting, and if he indeed were a woman, many people would never give him a second glance.

> *How often do you make snap judgments about others based on appearances? How often do you think others make similar judgments about you? When was the last time you discovered there was more to a person than you initially thought?*

LUKE 7:44-47

Then Jesus turned toward the woman and said to Simon, "Do you see this woman? I came into your house. You did not give me any water for my feet, but she wet my feet with her tears and wiped them with her hair. You did not give me a kiss, but this woman, from the time I entered, has not stopped kissing my feet. You did not put oil on my head, but she has poured perfume on my feet. Therefore, I tell you, her many sins have been forgiven—as her great love has shown. But whoever has been forgiven little loves little."

Simon the Pharisee was embarrassed that a notorious harlot would enter his house and make a spectacle of herself at the feet of Jesus. Simon was sure Jesus could not be a man of God or he would have known what manner of woman was touching him.

Jesus saw something entirely different in the woman. He saw her tears as a sign of the grace of God that had already begun to transform her life. Her actions were the only way she knew to express her profound gratitude for the grace shown to her. What she appeared to be on the surface was far different than what she was in her heart.

Simon was also different than he appeared on the surface. As a Pharisee, he was highly respected as a pillar of the community, but his heart was full of pride, self-righteousness and a critical spirit.

The woman was drawn to Jesus because he embodied the grace of God to her. Do you know anyone people are drawn to with the hope of finding love and grace? Do you know anyone people avoid from fear of criticism or condemnation? What makes the difference?

FOR REFLECTION AND DISCUSSION

To the extent you are comfortable doing so, share with your group your responses to the above questions and the following:

How many people did you look at critically this past week?

How often did you stop to consider what might be going on in the life of someone you looked at critically?

PRAYER

Open my eyes, Lord, to look beyond outward appearances and see what is in each person's heart. Thank you for the undeserved grace you have shown to me. Help me extend that same undeserved grace to others.

2.3 SEEING GOD'S IMAGE

While working on this book, my wife and I went to see *12 Years a Slave*, a movie based on an 1853 memoir of the same name. It tells the story of Solomon Northrup, who was born free in New York, kidnapped in Washington, D.C. and sold into slavery in Louisiana.

What struck me so powerfully as I watched the film and reflected on it afterward was the dehumanization that lay at the heart of slavery. I couldn't even say the slaves in the film were treated like animals because on our farm we would never have treated our animals so cruelly. Then again, our farm animals "knew their place" and caused no trouble, while slaves dared to believe they were human.

Dehumanization happens anytime we imagine people to be something less than created in God's image with hearts and souls and minds like our own. Unfortunately, this happens far too often, and when we treat others as less than human, we become less than human ourselves. It is the way we fight wars, run prisons and engage in politics. It is not the way God created us.

GENESIS 1:26-27

Then God said, "Let us make mankind in our image, in our likeness, so that they may rule over the fish in the sea and the birds in the sky, over the livestock and all the wild animals, and over all the creatures that move along the ground."

Step Two: Seeing

*So God created mankind in his own image,
in the image of God he created them;
male and female he created them.*

What does it mean to be human? What is the nature of God? The overlap between answers to these two questions lies at the heart of what Genesis describes as mankind being made in God's image.

It is helpful to remember the first part of what Jesus called the Great Commandment: love God with all your heart, all your soul and all your mind. As humans, we share these three things with God.

- **Heart *(feeling)*** – *experiencing joy, sorrow, peace, anger, awe, beauty, goodness, compassion and a full range of emotions*
- **Soul *(doing)*** – *choosing between alternatives and using the resources at our disposal to give shape to our lives and to the world around us*
- **Mind *(thinking)*** – *understanding complex ideas and situations; imagining the future consequences of our actions and planning accordingly*

There are other parts of creation that reflect God's image, but none to the extent that humans do. This does not make us gods, but it does allow a connection with our Creator that no other part of creation is capable of experiencing.

Besides feeling, doing and thinking, what attributes might be included in the "image of God" in which you were created?

How often do you give thanks to God for the miracle of your own life and the abilities you have?

GENESIS 3:1-7

Now the serpent was more crafty than any of the wild animals the Lord God had made. He said to the woman, "Did God really say, 'You must not eat from any tree in the garden'?"

The woman said to the serpent, "We may eat fruit from the trees in the garden, but God did say, 'You must not eat fruit from the tree that is in the middle of the garden, and you must not touch it, or you will die.'"

"You will not certainly die," the serpent said to the woman. "For God knows that when you eat from it your eyes will be opened, and you will be like God, knowing good and evil."

When the woman saw that the fruit of the tree was good for food and pleasing to the eye, and also desirable for gaining wisdom, she took some and ate it. She also gave some to her husband, who was with her, and he ate it. Then the eyes of both of them were opened, and they realized they were naked...

Eating the forbidden fruit may have opened their eyes, but it made the image of God in them harder and harder to see:

- **Heart (*feeling*)** – *they sought peace, joy and love, but so often they found just the opposite as they lived with their shame and guilt*
- ***Soul (doing)*** – *they chose to disobey God's clear command and the consequences were huge: they lost the peace of the garden and soon experienced grief and loss as one of their sons killed the other*
- ***Mind (thinking)*** – *they grasped "worldly wisdom" that showed them how to get everything they wanted even as it led them away from God*

Although Adam and Eve's fall from grace obscured the image of God in them, God never stopped loving them. For instance, even though Adam and Eve forfeited their right to live in the Garden of Eden, God made leather clothes for them before they went out into the wilderness (see Genesis 3:21). Like a parent, God was telling his children "You can't go out there dressed like that!"

No matter how obscured it may be, the image of God remains in every person; no one is beyond God's love. When we have trouble seeing something worthwhile in a person, we need to stop and ask, "God, what do you see in this person to love?"

> *Have you ever been repelled by a bad attitude or behavior in someone only to discover later something good in them?*
>
> *What kind of attitudes or behavior most obscure the image of God in people? How can you get past that to see God's image?*

FOR REFLECTION AND DISCUSSION

To the extent you are comfortable doing so, share with your group your responses to the above questions and the following:
Did you look differently at someone this week?

PRAYER

Thank you, God, for the wonderful way you have made each one of us. Make me more like Jesus in order that I may see your image in others and they might see your image in me.

2.4 SEEING POSSIBILITIES

I will never forget a story told me by Paul Ethington, a good friend from Green Lake, Wisconsin. He was director of Camp Grow at the time and had gone through a really tough period dealing with cancer and a broken back sustained in a fall. As if health issues weren't enough, the Camp was in the midst of a financial crisis and Paul was having trouble finding the right staff for the approaching season.

In the midst of praying for all these concerns and feeling more than a little desperate, he suddenly had an image of God saying to him in a panicked voice, "Oh no, Paul, what are we going to do?"

The ridiculousness of this image touched Paul deeply and he realized God was far from overwhelmed by these problems. Then a new image came to Paul and he heard God quietly say, "Trust me."

Paul told me he and the camp not only survived the crisis, but he experienced a profound peace while going through it.

In the midst of a problem, it is tempting to ask, "How did I get into this mess?" This often devolves into trying to figure out who to blame, and it almost never solves anything.

The alternative to this generally unhelpful approach is to ask a very different question: "What can I do now?" The first question may bring the satisfaction of placing blame, but it is almost always the second question that makes it possible to move forward.

JOHN 9:1-5

As Jesus went along, he saw a man blind from birth. His disciples asked him, "Rabbi, who sinned, this man or his parents, that he was born blind?"

"Neither this man nor his parents sinned," said Jesus, "but this happened so that the works of God might be displayed in him. As long as it is day, we must do the works of him who sent me. Night is coming, when no one can work. While I am in the world, I am the light of the world."

When the disciples looked at this man who had been blind from birth, they like everyone else saw someone who was clearly to be pitied. After all, it seemed patently unfair to them that he should be punished by God in this way either for sins he had committed in the womb or for the sin his parents must have committed before he was born.

Jesus told the disciples they were looking at this all wrong. The man's blindness was not a punishment for sin, but an opportunity for the love of God to be put into practice.

When you see someone suffering, do you get hung up on asking why something like this happens?

Some will say to those who are suffering, "This is all part of God's plan." Is such an idea true? Is it helpful? What could you say instead?

MATTHEW 16:21-23

From that time on Jesus began to explain to his disciples that he must go to Jerusalem and suffer many things at the hands of the elders, the chief priests and the teachers of the law, and that he must be killed and on the third day be raised to life.

Peter took him aside and began to rebuke him. "Never, Lord!" he said. "This shall never happen to you!"

Jesus turned and said to Peter, "Get behind me, Satan! You are a stumbling block to me; you do not have in mind the concerns of God, but merely human concerns."

Peter can hardly be blamed for reacting the way he did; it was simply unthinkable the destiny of Jesus would be to suffer and die rather than rule the nation as God's Messiah.

Even Jesus struggled with this. Just hours before his arrest and trial, he was still asking God if there might not be a way to avoid the suffering that was to come. As Luke 22:42 records it, Jesus prayed, "Father, if you are willing, take this cup from me; yet not my will, but yours be done."

Jesus knew following God would bring him suffering, but he also knew it was the best way to go. He knew even when the situation was bad, God was good.

How do you react to hard times and challenges? Have you ever had a bad situation lead to something better than expected?

How do you feel when people "encourage" you by telling you everything will work out okay in the end?

FOR REFLECTION AND DISCUSSION

To the extent you are comfortable doing so, share with your group your responses to the above questions.

PRAYER

Forgive me, Lord, for always wanting to know why things happen. Give me the sense of your abiding presence as I trust you to show me what to do when my life or someone else's is falling apart.

Ministry Reflections

Recognizing the ministry context of your life is an essential part of learning to love your neighbor. The following questions based on the lessons in this section can be discussed at each week's meeting or in a separate session later.

1. *Did you find yourself looking critically at people because of how they looked or acted?*

2. *Did you see something in someone that surprised you because it was not what you expected based on the person's appearance?*

3. *Did you see the image of God in someone? What negative thinking, bitter feelings, selfish actions or other distortions made it most difficult for you to see God's image in people?*

4. *Did you see an opportunity to show God's love to someone who was going through a hard time? Was the response what you expected it to be?*

STEP THREE: LISTENING

For many of us, listening doesn't come easily because we would much rather speak and let others listen to us.

It took me a long time to learn that the greatest ministry to someone in crisis is often nothing more than our non-anxious presence. Words may ring hollow, but simply being with people in their darkest hour can bring healing and hope even if little is said.

When I was in the midst of a crisis, Jack and Jane Riddle, a wonderful couple from church, invited me over. Jack said, "Come for dinner. If you want to talk, we'll talk. If you want to watch a ball game, we'll watch a ball game. Whatever works for you will work for us." I gratefully accepted Jack's invitation and told him how much I appreciated their sensitivity. I had no idea whether I would want to talk or not, but knowing I would be warmly welcomed by this gracious couple meant the world to me.

Listening is also at the heart of our relationship with God. It is easy for prayer to become a religious version of a child's Christmas letter to Santa: "Dear God, I want..." How much better to listen in order to hear what God wants.

Mother Teresa explained her life of prayer to a reporter in an elegantly simple way:

Reporter: "What is the secret of your success?"

Mother Teresa: "I spend much time in prayer."

Reporter: "What do you say to God?"

Mother Teresa: "Nothing. I just listen."

Reporter: "Then what does God say to you?"

Mother Teresa: "Nothing. God just listens."

Step Three: Listening

I love Mother Teresa's image of prayer: spending time with God and listening to each other in the silence of the moment. A silent presence can be wonderfully intimate and comforting.

May the following lessons help you grow in your ability and desire to listen to God and to the people God has placed in your life.

3.1 LISTENING TO GOD

Something remarkable happened on a Sunday morning in the summer of 1983, a time when I was pastor of a small church and my marriage was falling apart. As I sat in my office trying to figure out if my sermon was ready, I received a devastating phone call from my then wife.

When the call ended, I was a total mess. I couldn't imagine leading the worship service that was supposed to start in less than an hour. I sat there immobilized until the phone rang again. The man on the other end was Press Webster, an old friend who was now a pastor in southern Illinois. What he said still rings in my ears decades later:

"I don't know what's happening in your life these days, Dave, but as I was praying this morning, your name came to mind. God has shown me when this happens, I should do something about it. I'm just calling to let you know how much I love you and how much God loves you. I'm praying you will have a great worship service this morning."

I was crying so hard throughout his call that I'm not sure I actually said anything, but I knew I had just received about as personal a message from God as anyone ever could.

I don't remember what my sermon was like that morning and I was soon forced to face the fact my marriage wouldn't survive, but God healed my life and my ministry that day in a way I will never forget. I have no idea in what direction my life would have gone if Press hadn't been listening to God.

The Bible has many stories of God being intimately involved in people's lives, speaking to them and leading them in their interactions with others.

ACTS 8:27-31

So (Philip) started out, and on his way he met an Ethiopian eunuch, an important official in charge of all the treasury of the Kandake (which means "queen of the Ethiopians"). This man had gone to Jerusalem to worship, and on his way home was sitting in his chariot reading the Book of Isaiah the prophet. The Spirit told Philip, "Go to that chariot and stay near it."

Then Philip ran up to the chariot and heard the man reading Isaiah the prophet. "Do you understand what you are reading?" Philip asked.

"How can I," he said, "unless someone explains it to me?" So he invited Philip to come up and sit with him.

Philip and the Ethiopian eunuch had little in common other than God working in their lives. Notice what Philip did:

- He was *led* by the Spirit to talk to the man.
- He *went* to the man rather than waiting for the man to come to him.
- He *heard* the man reading from Isaiah.
- He *offered* to help the man understand.

After his encounter with Philip, the Ethiopian Eunuch was baptized and went on his way rejoicing.

Have you ever been led by the Spirit to speak to someone? Would you be willing to do this if you were confident it was God's Spirit leading you?

LUKE 19:2-10

A man was there by the name of Zacchaeus; he was a chief tax collector and was wealthy. He wanted to see who Jesus was, but because he was short he could not see over the crowd. So he ran ahead and climbed a sycamore-fig tree to see him, since Jesus was coming that way.

When Jesus reached the spot, he looked up and said to him, "Zacchaeus, come down immediately. I must stay at your house today." So he came down at once and welcomed him gladly.

All the people saw this and began to mutter, "He has gone to be the guest of a sinner."

But Zacchaeus stood up and said to the Lord, "Look, Lord! Here and now I give half of my possessions to the poor, and if I have cheated anybody out of anything, I will pay back four times the amount."

Jesus said to him, "Today salvation has come to this house, because this man, too, is a son of Abraham. For the Son of Man came to seek and to save the lost."

It is possible that Jesus had some prior relationship with Zacchaeus, but the only thing we know for sure is that Jesus invited himself over for dinner to the home of a man who was hated by almost everyone.

Tax collectors were despised by the Jews as traitors because they were Jews who collected taxes on behalf of Rome. They were also considered to be crooks because they purchased their positions with the understanding that they could keep whatever taxes they collected above what Rome demanded. The tax collector's profit was thus the tax payer's loss. As chief tax collector, Zacchaeus would have profited greatly from the entire corrupt system.

Jesus would have been most unlikely to have moved toward Zacchaeus unless God was leading him in the same way Philip was led to speak to the Ethiopian Eunuch. In both cases, the results were dramatic.

Zacchaeus wanted to meet Jesus, but was amazed Jesus wanted to meet him. Do you think of your story as one of finding Jesus or of being found by him?

FOR REFLECTION AND DISCUSSION

To the extent that you are comfortable doing so, share with the group your responses to the above questions.

PRAYER

When you lead me, Lord, I can connect even with people who have nothing in common with me and no obvious connection with you. Give me the wisdom and courage I need to follow where you lead.

3.2 LISTENING FOR GOD

I'm not sure where it began, but for much of my life I've been under the impression that most people have little or no interest in God. Operating with that assumption, evangelism for me became trying to sell people something I was convinced they didn't really want.

God has shown me otherwise. One morning I was sitting in my office when the phone rang. The man introduced himself as Dave and told me he might end his life if I couldn't help him. I asked him to tell me his story.

Dave had been on a drug binge for several days and had spent everything. Worse than that, he had given his wife's car to a drug dealer as collateral when all his money was gone. Dave told me unless he could come up with $60 that morning, his wife would have no way to get to work and would lose her job. Dave had lost his job because of drug issues and his wife was the sole support of Dave and their three children.

As a pastor, I had been approached countless times for help and was always suspicious when someone said the only help they needed was cash. Still, I took $60 with me and offered to meet Dave to hear more of his story.

A short time later, Dave and I were headed into the Projects to find Snake, his drug dealer. When I told my wife later what I had done, she was shocked to say the least. I had never before knowingly met a drug dealer, but I went with Dave because I knew God was leading me to do so.

When the dealer opened the door, Dave introduced me as a pastor who was helping him and Snake replied, "I'm so glad you're doing that. Dave is kind of messed up and needs God in his life. While you're at it, maybe you could pray for me."

I was probably as astounded by what the drug dealer said as he was to see a pastor standing at his door. I'm not sure if either of these guys was ready to follow Jesus, but it certainly looked like God was doing something in their lives. Sometimes we can see and hear God at work in the most unlikely places if we will only open our eyes and ears.

LUKE 23:39-43

One of the criminals who hung there hurled insults at him: "Aren't you the Messiah? Save yourself and us!"

But the other criminal rebuked him. "Don't you fear God," he said, "since you are under the same sentence? We are punished justly, for we are getting what our deeds deserve. But this man has done nothing wrong." Then he said, "Jesus, remember me when you come into your kingdom."

Jesus answered him, "Truly I tell you, today you will be with me in paradise."

The two men crucified with Jesus were not petty criminals even if tradition refers to them as thieves. Crucifixion was only for those convicted of the most serious offenses.

How differently the two criminals looked at Jesus. One saw him as the coming king; the other saw only a deluded man who would die a fool.

Jesus also had a unique perspective on the criminals. The world saw them as worthless men getting the punishment they deserved. Jesus looked beyond a life of detestable crime to see God at work in at least one of them.

It is remarkable that it was a criminal, not a disciple, who first grasped the possibility of a crucified king coming into a kingdom.

> *Had you been there, how might you have looked at the criminals on the cross? How might you have looked at Jesus?*
>
> *When you see the worst criminals today, can you imagine God working in their lives to draw them to himself?*

MARK 12:28-34

One of the teachers of the law came and heard them debating. Noticing that Jesus had given them a good answer, he asked him, "Of all the commandments, which is the most important?"

"The most important one," answered Jesus, "is this: 'Hear, O Israel: The Lord our God, the Lord is one. Love the Lord your God with all your heart and with all your soul and with all your mind and with all your strength.' The second is this: 'Love your neighbor as yourself.' There is no commandment greater than these."

"Well said, teacher," the man replied. "You are right in saying that God is one and there is no other but him. To love him with all your heart, with all your understanding and with all your strength, and to love your neighbor as yourself is more important than all burnt offerings and sacrifices."

When Jesus saw that he had answered wisely, he said to him, "You are not far from the kingdom of God." And from then on no one dared ask him any more questions.

The two groups most strongly opposed to Jesus were the Pharisees and the Scribes, the latter often referred to as "religious lawyers" or "teachers of the Law." This story shows how Jesus at times saw God at work even in the lives of his fiercest opponents.

> *Have you ever seen God working in the life of someone from a different denomination or religion? Were you surprised?*

FOR REFLECTION AND DISCUSSION

To the extent that you are comfortable doing so, share with the group your responses to the above questions.

PRAYER

Open my eyes, Lord, to see you as you are and to see others as they could be if only they were to come face to face with your transforming love.

3.3 Listening to Pain

Tom Roberts is the pastor of a wonderful church, though when he arrived there six years ago, it had a very different reputation. Back then it was known as a church that was hard on pastors.

I asked Tom how the church turned around so dramatically and he said it was simple: "When I came here everyone was angry, but I soon discovered everyone was hurting. I spent a lot of time that first year or two just listening to people, letting them tell me what they were angry about and in the process learning where they were hurting. God's love and grace brought healing to the pain in their lives and everything changed."

Here it was: a simple solution to a common problem that few were willing to tackle. Jesus did much the same thing, meeting people who were angry, hurt, discouraged and afraid, then letting them talk and listening to what they were saying before offering them hope and healing.

John 5:5-9

One who was there had been an invalid for thirty-eight years. When Jesus saw him lying there and learned that he had been in this condition for a long time, he asked him, "Do you want to get well?"

"Sir," the invalid replied, "I have no one to help me into the pool when the water is stirred. While I am trying to get in, someone else goes down ahead of me."

Then Jesus said to him, "Get up! Pick up your mat and walk."
At once the man was cured; he picked up his mat and
walked.

Jesus *saw* this man among all the others waiting at the pool to be healed. Sometimes God's Spirit leads us to specific people, preparing the way for us to meet them.

Jesus *learned* this man's history, becoming familiar with the man's situation before speaking to him.

Jesus *asked* if the man wanted to be healed, a question that seemed to have an obvious answer, but not necessarily.

Jesus *healed* the man of the infirmity that had kept him incapacitated for most his life.

Do you find it easy or difficult to get people to tell you about themselves? Is it helpful to learn a person's story by asking others about them?

Can you imagine that God might use you to bring hope and healing to someone?

MARK 10:46-52 (NRSV)

They came to Jericho. As he and his disciples and a large crowd were leaving Jericho, Bartimaeus son of Timaeus, a blind beggar, was sitting by the roadside. When he heard that it was Jesus of Nazareth, he began to shout out and say, "Jesus, Son of David, have mercy on me!" Many sternly ordered him to be quiet, but he cried out even more loudly, "Son of David, have mercy on me!" Jesus stood still and said, "Call him here." And they called the blind man, saying to him, "Take heart; get up, he is calling you." So throwing off his cloak, he sprang up and came to Jesus. Then Jesus said to him, "What do you want me to do for you?" The blind man said to him, "My teacher, let me see again." Jesus said to him, "Go; your faith has made you well." Immediately he regained his sight and followed him on the way

Jesus could have asked the man why he was shouting so loudly and persistently. He could have asked him what had happened to make him blind. Instead, Jesus had but one simple question, "What do you want me to do for you?"

> *The crowd tried to get the desperate man to stop shouting. Who do we try to silence today? Do we get annoyed with people who won't "shut up" about their problems?*

FOR REFLECTION AND DISCUSSION

To the extent you are comfortable doing so, share with the group your responses to the above questions and the following:

Did you have an opportunity this week to ask someone, "What do you really want?"

PRAYER

Jesus, you knew just the right thing to say and do in every situation. Help me follow your lead when I feel awkward in my attempts to be helpful. Hold me back from trying to silence the cries of the desperate; remind me to ask instead what it is they truly want.

3.4 LISTENING FOR PAIN

When I was starting out in ministry, an older pastor told me if I assumed each person in worship on Sunday morning was suffering in some way, I would be right more often than wrong.

Society teaches people to hide their pain. Some pretend everything is alright out of shame while others stay quiet out of hopelessness. They believe it is useless to speak since no one can do anything about their problems anyway. Still others dread the way people will try to fix their problems and make them feel better.

Naomi Rachel Remen, author of *Kitchen Table Wisdom* and *My Grandfather's Blessings*, has much to say about the healing that comes from listening.

> The most basic and powerful way to connect to another person is to listen. Just listen.... A loving silence often has far more power to heal and to connect than the most well-intentioned words...not the sort of silence that is filled with unspoken criticism or hard withdrawal. The sort of silence that is a place of refuge, of rest, of acceptance of someone as they are. We are all hungry for this other silence. It is hard to find. In its presence we can remember something beyond the moment, a strength on which to build a life. Silence is a place of great power and healing."

JOHN 4:7-9

When a Samaritan woman came to draw water, Jesus said to her, "Will you give me a drink?" (His disciples had gone

71

into the town to buy food.)

The Samaritan woman said to him, "You are a Jew and I am a Samaritan woman. How can you ask me for a drink?" (For Jews do not associate with Samaritans.)

Jesus listened to what the woman said, but also to what she didn't say; there was pain in each.

She didn't speak of pain, but her acknowledgment of Jewish dislike of Samaritans indicated it was there. She might as well have said angrily, "I thought to Jews like you, we Samaritans were nothing more than dirt beneath your feet." Those who feel pain often express anger.

She also said nothing about why she came to the well in the heat of the day rather than in the cooler dawn or twilight hours. Coming when no one else was there would help the woman escape the snide remarks and cruel comments of those familiar with her personal life.

> *Think of someone you know who has anger issues. How much of that anger stems from the person being hurt at some point? What could you do to help someone who is angry deal with underlying pain?*

JOHN 4:13-19

Jesus answered, "Everyone who drinks this water will be thirsty again, but whoever drinks the water I give them will never thirst. Indeed, the water I give them will become in them a spring of water welling up to eternal life."

The woman said to him, "Sir, give me this water so that I won't get thirsty and have to keep coming here to draw water."

He told her, "Go, call your husband and come back."

"I have no husband," she replied.

Jesus said to her, "You are right when you say you have no husband. The fact is, you have had five husbands, and the man you now have is not your husband. What you have just said is quite true."

"Sir," the woman said, "I can see that you are a prophet."

Jesus continued the conversation with the Samaritan woman by beginning to connect her story with God's story: she knew the drudgery of coming every day to the well for water; he spoke of a living water that would satisfy fully and forever.

Still, there was more pain in the woman's life that had not yet been given expression. When asked to bring her husband to Jesus, she responded with a truth that was not the whole truth. She was still wary of Jesus and uncertain whether he could be trusted with the painful details of her life.

Jesus responded in a manner showing he understood more of her story than she imagined, and yet betrayed no judgment or condemnation on his part. The more Jesus acknowledged her pain, the more she was willing to admit.

Are you the kind of non-judgmental person with whom people regularly share the details of their life?

What might you do to provide a safe place for people to share things they are generally hesitant to reveal?

FOR REFLECTION AND DISCUSSION

To the extent that you are comfortable doing so, share with the group your responses to the above questions.

PRAYER

Help me be tuned in, Lord, to the pain in people's lives. Help me hear what is unsaid and see what is hidden in order that the light of your love might shine in their darkness. Fill my heart with compassion rather than judgment.

MINISTRY REFLECTIONS

Participation in a ministry context is an essential part of "Learning to Love Your Neighbor." The following questions based on the lessons in this section can be discussed at each week's meeting or in a separate session later.

1. *Did you sense God leading you to talk with a particular person this month? Did you have a "coincidental" encounter with someone that led to a meaningful connection?*

2. *Did you see God at work in someone's life this month in a surprising way? Did you discover spiritual interests in a person you thought had none?*

3. *Did you listen this month to someone's noisy complaints? Did you have an opportunity to ask, "What do you want?"*

4. *Did you listen this month to the story of someone who was hurting? Were you able to offer a loving presence while resisting the urge to offer platitudes, clichés or easy answers?*

Learning to Love Your Neighbor

STEP FOUR:
SERVING

I remember the first Garage Sale my wife, Linnea, and I had. Because there was so much stuff, we spent way more time than we wanted figuring out how to price each item. What particularly bothered us was knowing people would haggle over the price no matter what it was. Some people enjoy the game of garage sale haggling; we don't.

It all came to a head when someone brought me an item priced at $.25 and asked if I would take less. I don't even remember what the item was, but I do remember saying in a voice that was not overly charitable, "No. I will not take less, but I will give it to you for nothing!"

After reflecting on this experience, I realized two things: 1) I had been wrong to speak unkindly to the woman who offered me less, and 2) I actually enjoyed giving her the item for nothing.

Thus was born the idea for a Priceless Garage Sale. Every item would be available for any donation and all proceeds would go to One Great Hour of Sharing, a disaster relief program of our church. This was a win-win-win program: we got rid of stuff we no longer wanted or needed; buyers got something they wanted for the price they wanted; and people around the world were helped in times of crisis.

It was not long before the Priceless Garage Sale idea spread and it became an annual church-wide event. We had no trouble gathering plenty of items for the sale and drawing a big crowd. The only problem we had was with the cash box. I soon realized some church people became frustrated when anyone gave less than an item was worth. I cringed when a cashier tried to shame a person into giving more: "Come on. It's for a good cause and you know it's worth more than that."

How quickly a moment of grace can become a moment of guilt.

In reflecting the heart of God, Jesus was extravagant with his demonstrations of unconditional love. By contrast, we typically base our love and generosity on what we think people deserve. Loving only those we think are worthy is deeply ingrained in us. This makes it hard to grasp the concept of unconditional love for the unworthy and undeserving.

One of the best examples of unconditional love comes from the musical, *Les Mis*. The hero, Jean Valjean, suffered long years at hard labor in prison for stealing a loaf of bread to feed a starving child. Upon his release, he became a thief because his identity as a convicted felon made it impossible for him to get honest work.

Valjean is offered refuge in the home of a kindly Bishop and before the night is over steals from him. Caught by the police, Valjean argues that the items were given him by the Bishop. When questioned, the Bishop not only backs Valjean's story but chastises him for leaving the most valuable gifts behind.

Such unexpected and undeserved grace shown to a man who had until then known only abuse and mistreatment became life-changing. Valjean's new life began with that act of grace.

It is my hope that *Learning to Love Your Neighbor* will allow you to experience the joy of seeing new life in someone who discovers God's love and grace through you.

4.1 Serving Jesus

When I was 30 years old, I was living and working at Northern Seminary in the Chicago area. I remember one cold winter day a homeless man was walking to the campus from a nearby shopping mall. He asked if he could sit in our lobby for a few minutes to warm up and I said it would be fine.

As he sat down, I couldn't help but notice how worn his shoes were. Each sole had a sizable hole in it and I could see he had used newspapers to provide at least some insulation against the cold. The paper wasn't much help, though, given the considerable snow on the ground.

I asked what size he wore and he confirmed he wore about the same size I did. I went to my apartment to find my winter boots. They were almost new because I had other shoes and boots I could wear except on the coldest days.

When I came back and gave the man my shoes, I could see he was more than pleased. He put them on, went on his way and I never saw him again.

I wish I had talked with him more in order to hear his story, but I had other priorities that day. Maybe all he needed was some warm shoes, and maybe that was all I had to give.

Jesus identified with those who were poor and needy so completely that he said serving them was the same as serving him. The scene described below is the judgment that comes when Jesus returns at the end of the age.

MATTHEW 25:37-40

"Then the righteous will answer him, 'Lord, when did we see you hungry and feed you, or thirsty and give you something to drink? When did we see you a stranger and invite you in, or needing clothes and clothe you? When did we see you sick or in prison and go to visit you?'

"The King will reply, 'Truly I tell you, whatever you did for one of the least of these brothers and sisters of mine, you did for me.'

In this passage, Jesus identifies in a remarkable way with all who suffer. Given what Jesus experienced, perhaps his connection with our suffering shouldn't surprise us.

Jesus knew what it was to be hungry. He fasted forty days in the desert and resisted the temptation to turn stones into bread. Later he had compassion on the multitudes, providing bread and fish to 5,000 people one time and 4,000 another.

Do you find joy in providing a good meal to friends and family? Do you find joy in feeding strangers?

How many people in your community go hungry on a regular basis? Does it bother you not to know the answer to that question?

Jesus knew what it was to be thirsty. At a Samaritan well, he asked a woman for a drink. On the cross, he said, "I am thirsty" just before saying his last words: "It is finished."

The USA generally has good, healthy water available through wells and water systems. The same cannot be said for much of the rest of the world. Contaminated water produces diarrhea and is one of the five leading causes of death worldwide, ending 3 million lives each year, 60% of which are children.

> *How much do you spend in a month on bottled water, soda pop, coffee, tea, beer, wine and other beverages? Would you give up these for a month and donate what you save to a charity that provides clean water to those who have none?*

Jesus knew what it meant to be considered a stranger, even among his own people.[2] "Stranger" can have many meanings: outsider, foreigner, immigrant, alien, sojourner, refugee, traveler, homeless. At different points in his life, Jesus was all of these. He was homeless at his birth and, when threatened by Herod, became a refugee immigrant in Egypt.

> *Do American attitudes about illegal immigrants and the emphasis on "stranger-danger" affect your understanding of what Jesus says about inviting "strangers" into your home?*

Jesus knew what it was to be stripped of his clothes. As he was dying on the cross, soldiers gambled for what he wore, believing Jesus' robe was more valuable than he was. Through the generosity of Joseph of Arimathea, the nakedness of Jesus was covered before his burial.

> *How full is your closet? Do you hold on to clothes you are no longer willing or able to wear, or do you give them away to someone who needs them more than you?*

---

[2] See John 1:11

Jesus knew what it meant to suffer physical affliction. He may never have had cancer or even a tension headache, but he agonized as he prayed in the garden, felt terrible pain as the crown of thorns was pressed down upon his head and was beaten brutally before his crucifixion. Jesus' body felt pain like ours; his suffering was no less than our own.

> *When you hear someone is sick, do you tend to go to them or avoid them? Do you find yourself drained by the chronic illnesses of others?*

Jesus knew what it meant to be imprisoned with no one to visit him. His closest friends abandoned him when he was arrested; he faced his trial all alone.

Those who have spent time in prison rarely find it easy to re-enter society. Their résumé has an obvious hole in it from time incarcerated and personal references are not easy to secure. Few employers give ex-prisoners a chance and rules automatically eliminate them from consideration for many jobs.

> *In Les Mis, Jean Valjean says to his jailer, Jauvert, "I am a man like any other." Do you see criminals as being somehow different from "normal" people?*
>
> *What personal interactions have you had with anyone who has spent time in prison? Have you ever visited someone there?*

FOR REFLECTION AND DISCUSSION

To the extent you are comfortable doing so, share with your group your responses to the above questions and the following:

How would it impact your attitude about serving those in need if you were able to understand how doing so was a way of serving Jesus?

PRAYER

Heavenly Father, help me show concern for your hungry and thirsty children. Help me receive strangers and outsiders with the same warm welcome I would give Jesus. Forgive me for those times I imagine the sins of those in prison to be much worse than my own.

4.2 SERVING OUTSIDERS

I remember it as though it was yesterday and yet it happened nearly 50 years ago.

I was home from college for the summer and working for my dad on the farm. One day when it was raining too hard to work in the fields, I spent the afternoon reading a book of sermons by Peter Marshall.

I don't remember the sermon's title, but the text was the Luke 14:12-18 passage that appears below. Dr. Marshall put the story in a modern context, describing a wealthy man who sent his butler to the worst part of the city with engraved cards inviting people to a dinner given in honor of Jesus of Nazareth.

Not surprisingly, those who received the invitations were skeptical. Some decided they had nothing to lose and accepted. A limousine stopped by to pick them up at the appointed hour.

When the wonderful meal was over, the guests pressed their host for an explanation of what his angle was. The man said he had no angle, but was simply carrying out the wishes of his master, Jesus of Nazareth.

As I read the sermon, I began to weep as never before. I could only think, "Is it possible that life could actually be lived this way?"

Peter Marshall's sermon gave me my first glimpse of God's kingdom in which love and shalom (peace and well-being) ruled the day. It was a turning point in my life as I began to see what my place in God's plan to fix a broken world might be.

LUKE 14:12-15

Then Jesus said to his host, "When you give a luncheon or dinner, do not invite your friends, your brothers or sisters, your relatives, or your rich neighbors; if you do, they may invite you back and so you will be repaid. But when you give a banquet, invite the poor, the crippled, the lame, the blind, and you will be blessed. Although they cannot repay you, you will be repaid at the resurrection of the righteous."

When one of those at the table with him heard this, he said to Jesus, "Blessed is the one who will eat at the feast in the kingdom of God."

The kingdom of God has often been referred to as the "upside down" kingdom because it is in so many ways the opposite of our own world.

The social custom in Jesus' day (and in ours) was based on "one good turn deserves another." Such thinking encourages us to help those who have helped us in the past and may do so again in the future.

The closing comment by one of those eating with Jesus was a way of saying, "Surely such wretched people will have no part at the feast in the kingdom of God!" Read Luke 14:16-24 to see the story Jesus told in response.

What would it look like for you to take seriously what Jesus says to do here? What problems might arise if you invited into your home those who could never return the favor?

FOR REFLECTION AND DISCUSSION

To the extent you are comfortable doing so, share with your group your responses to the above questions and the following:

Is there a service project your group could do together and talk about afterward? This would be a wonderful chance for you to step outside your normal circles and put into practice what you have been learning about seeing, listening and serving.

PRAYER

Help me break through cultural norms, Lord, to glimpse what your kingdom could look like in today's world.

4.3 SERVING UNTOUCHABLES

In my early years of pastoral ministry, I have to admit I was a little bit envious of people in the hospital. I thought it might be nice to get as much sleep as you wanted and have people wait on you for everything.

Then I was hospitalized and discovered it wasn't at all like I had imagined. There was noise in the hallway all night and so much beeping in my room that sleep was just about impossible. When I did manage to sleep, someone would inevitably come by to draw blood and check my vital signs or do something else that left me wide awake.

I also noticed doctors and nurses washing and gloving their hands before and after examining me. I knew this was for my safety as well as their own, and yet I couldn't help feeling like an untouchable whenever it happened.

Many of the people Jesus healed had lived as untouchables for years. Those touching a person who was ritually unclean due to leprosy, menstruation or a number of other ailments became unclean themselves through contamination. In the healings by Jesus, however, the unclean were "contaminated" with cleanness and the sick with health.

MATTHEW 8:1-4

When Jesus came down from the mountainside, large crowds followed him. A man with leprosy came and knelt before him and said, "Lord, if you are willing, you can make me clean."

Jesus reached out his hand and touched the man. "I am willing," he said. "Be clean!" Immediately he was cleansed of his leprosy. Then Jesus said to him, "See that you don't tell anyone. But go, show yourself to the priest and offer the gift Moses commanded, as a testimony to them."

Leviticus 13:45 specified that lepers were to cover their upper lips, avoid contact with all people and shout, "Unclean! Unclean!" to warn people away from them.

It must have taken great courage and faith for this man to approach and kneel before Jesus in the midst of such a crowd.

"If you are willing" was not said to question if Jesus had compassion, but as an expression of the man's profound sense of unworthiness.

Physical contact was not required for Jesus to heal, but for this leper the touch of Jesus brought more than physical healing.

What kind of things make someone feel like an untouchable today?

Would it be hard for you to speak to an untouchable today or to shake hands, hug or touch them in some way?

ACTS 3:2-8

Now a man who was lame from birth was being carried to the temple gate called Beautiful, where he was put every day to beg from those going into the temple courts. When he saw Peter and John about to enter, he asked them for money. Peter looked straight at him, as did John. Then Peter said, "Look at us!" So the man gave them his attention, expecting to get something from them.

Then Peter said, "Silver or gold I do not have, but what I do have I give you. In the name of Jesus Christ of Nazareth, walk." Taking him by the right hand, he helped him up, and instantly the man's feet and ankles became strong. He jumped to his feet and began to walk. Then he went with them into the temple courts, walking and jumping, and praising God.

The beggar hoped a few people entering the temple might give him a coin or two. He dared look no one in the eye lest he make someone so uncomfortable as to give him nothing. Few people noticed that he was even there; no one spoke to him.

Everything changed when Peter and John came along. Peter had no money to give, but he gave this beggar his full attention and brought healing as he grabbed this man's hand and lifted him up to new life.

Imagine that you, like Peter and John, encountered a beggar at the door of your church or in the streets of your community. What would you have to give this person in need?

Would you be more likely give the person a handout or offer them a handup?

FOR REFLECTION AND DISCUSSION

To the extent you are comfortable doing so, share with your group your responses to the above questions and the following:

Have you settled on a service project yet for your group?

PRAYER

Thank you, Lord, for the comforting touch of those who care. Help me be ready to give and to receive, focusing not on what I lack, but on what I have through you.

4.4 Serving Partners

Many church traditions mystify me. One is the requirement to be a member before participating in mission activities. I suspect there are some unstated assumptions involved here:

1. *Anyone who isn't a church member would have no interest in serving the poor.*

2. *Anyone who isn't a church member would have no idea how to serve the poor in a "Christian" manner.*

3. *If too many people who aren't church members help out, the church might not get the recognition it deserves for serving the poor.*

The first two assumptions are simply false and the third one is absolutely wrong because it betrays an entirely inappropriate motivation for serving.

As you feel led to serve, don't be surprised if God gives you opportunities for unlikely partnerships. For instance, you may find someone at work or a friend or neighbor who is interested in working with you at a homeless shelter. You may connect with teachers at the school or with staff at the nursing home where you get involved.

These partnerships are not a distraction from learning to love your neighbor; they may even play a central role in it. God is often at work in the lives of people in unexpected ways. The stories of a "good" Samaritan and a Philippian jailer show how love and mercy can come from surprising sources

Luke 10:30-35

In reply Jesus said: "A man was going down from Jerusalem to Jericho, when he was attacked by robbers. They stripped him of his clothes, beat him and went away, leaving him half dead. A priest happened to be going down the same road, and when he saw the man, he passed by on the other side. So too, a Levite, when he came to the place and saw him, passed by on the other side. But a Samaritan, as he traveled, came where the man was; and when he saw him, he took pity on him. He went to him and bandaged his wounds, pouring on oil and wine. Then he put the man on his own donkey, brought him to an inn and took care of him. The next day he took out two denarii and gave them to the innkeeper. 'Look after him,' he said, 'and when I return, I will reimburse you for any extra expense you may have.'

The lack of compassion by the priest and Levite brought no shame in Jesus' day; they were simply following the custom of avoiding those who were suffering in order not to be made unclean by coming in contact with them.

What is so extraordinary about the Samaritan is that he went out of his way to show compassion toward a man who in all likelihood would not have returned the favor. Jews had been prejudiced against Samaritans for hundreds of years. The very idea of "a good Samaritan" would have been shocking to any Jew.

How far would you go to help someone in distress if you knew the person's politics, religion or lifestyle were clearly at odds with your own?

Would you be willing to recruit for your ministry a person who doesn't share your faith?

ACTS 16:25-34

About midnight Paul and Silas were praying and singing hymns to God, and the other prisoners were listening to them. Suddenly there was such a violent earthquake that the foundations of the prison were shaken. At once all the prison doors flew open, and everyone's chains came loose.

The jailer woke up, and when he saw the prison doors open, he drew his sword and was about to kill himself because he thought the prisoners had escaped. But Paul shouted, "Don't harm yourself! We are all here!"

The jailer called for lights, rushed in and fell trembling before Paul and Silas. He then brought them out and asked, "Sirs, what must I do to be saved?"

They replied, "Believe in the Lord Jesus, and you will be saved—you and your household." Then they spoke the word of the Lord to him and to all the others in his house. At that hour of the night the jailer took them and washed their wounds; then immediately he and all his household were baptized. The jailer brought them into his house and set a meal before them; he was filled with joy because he had come to believe in God—he and his whole household.

The jailer's fear was well-founded: the escape of prisoners under his charge meant certain death for him.

The transformation in this man from jailer to servant was remarkable. He bathed the prisoners' wounds that had not only gone untended before, but may have been the result of abuse the jailer himself had inflicted. Then the jailer took them to his home, showing them gracious hospitality and serving them with a heart full of joy.

Paul and Silas could hardly have imagined that this jailer would go from being an enemy to being a servant in a matter of hours. It is amazing what God can do.

Have you ever seen God work in someone's life to turn them from an enemy into an ally? Would you be able to accept that if it did happen? What kind of assurances would you want that the person really had changed?

FOR REFLECTION AND DISCUSSION

To the extent you are comfortable doing so, share with the group your responses to the above questions and the following:

Have you worked together yet on a service project? Have you taken time to debrief each other on what you learned by doing it?

PRAYER

Give me the courage, Lord, to bathe the wounds of those I have hurt, and the grace to serve them in whatever way I can. And forgive me, Lord, for the times I let my love for others be constrained within the bounds of my pride and prejudice.

MINISTRY REFLECTIONS

For several months now you have been discovering how to minister to the people you meet in your daily life. This is all good, but the time comes when every bird must leave the comfortable nest and learn to fly.

Discuss as a group whether there is a service project you might want to undertake together. Let this be an opportunity to be led by Jesus and to see people through new eyes, listen to people's stories and serve them with the joy you would have in serving Jesus himself.

The following questions based on the lessons in this section can be discussed at each week's meeting or in a separate session later. They can be answered from the perspective of your ongoing ministry context or the one you have chosen to do as a group.

1. *Did you have a sense of seeing Jesus in someone who was hungry, thirsty, homeless, poorly dressed, sick or imprisoned? What was that like?*

2. *Did you have opportunity to serve someone who was a social outcast as the poor, the crippled, the lame and the blind would have been in Jesus' day? What was that like?*

3. *Did you connect with someone through a significant some conversation or interaction?*

4. *Did you discover a partner in ministry at the place where you are serving? Did this surprise you in some way?*

STEP FIVE: INVITING

When I began to think about college, I knew I would have to find either a school that was very inexpensive or one with an exceptional financial aid program. Crowder Junior College in my hometown of Neosho, Missouri fit well in the first category; I spent an afternoon in the library researching schools to see what might be in the second.

After reading about hundreds of schools, I discovered the best financial aid program in the country was at Harvard. I had never met anyone who had firsthand knowledge of it, but I certainly knew Harvard's reputation as one of the best colleges in the world. I applied, was admitted and received a scholarship that covered all my tuition and most of my room and board.

My parents were far less excited about this than I was. In fact, they strongly encouraged me not to go. Their concern was that I would be totally out of my element, an unwelcome "country boy" who was forever an outsider among all the rich kids who went there.

The decision was mine to make, though, because they were in no position to pay anything toward my education anyway. I took their concerns seriously, but ultimately decided to go for two reasons:

1. If it turned out badly, I could always come home and go to Crowder.
2. If I never gave it a chance, I would never know what it was like.

This line of thinking satisfied my parents and they began to be excited about the opportunity that awaited me.

To my joy and amazement, I quickly discovered at Harvard that I was warmly welcomed and fully accepted. The key factor was a sort of "Harvard hubris" that basically said, "Harvard never makes a mistake; if you are here you belong."

Before Harvard, I had always felt like an outsider. I grew up on a dairy farm, but never quite felt at home with other farm kids because my dad made it fairly clear that he wanted me to be anything but a farmer when I grew up; farming had been a hard life for him and he wanted something better for me.

I never quite felt at home with town kids either because I was a farmer. High school kids would invite me to do things with them, but I often had to decline because there were cows to be milked, fields to be plowed, hay to be baled or other work to be done. I didn't mind the work as much as I minded the missed opportunity to spend time with friends. Even when kids said they understood, I still felt like an outsider.

Jesus had a remarkable way of making outsiders and outcasts feel like they belonged. As we follow Jesus, we will find many opportunities to extend invitations to people. The lessons in this section focus on inviting people into *God's Story, God's Party, God's Family* and *God's Mission.* These are not the only invitations you are likely to give, but they are foundational ones.

For a list of examples, stories and various resources that may prove helpful as you learn to be a more inviting person, check out the website:

www.learningtoloveyourneighbor.com

5.1 INVITING INTO GOD'S STORY

My understanding of the Bible has certainly changed over the years. As a child I thought of it as a collection of unrelated stories about saints of old. As a young adult I saw it as filled with all the answers to life's questions if only I would commit its key verses to memory.

It wasn't until I studied the Bible seriously in seminary that I began to understand that it is actually the story of God's plan to redeem and recreate a world that has been pretty much destroyed by the disastrous choices people have made.

Unless we choose otherwise, we are all part of the problem described in the Bible as a world gone astray. After all, no one has to teach us to be self-centered, looking out for our own interests, taking vengeance on anyone who hurts us, and attacking anyone who gets in our way.

However, we can also be part of the answer because we are invited to be part of what God is doing. You may think few people have the necessary qualifications to be on God's team, but the Bible says otherwise. It is filled with stories of God working through some of the most unlikely people. The following stories are but a few examples.

LUKE 2:8-15

And there were shepherds living out in the fields nearby, keeping watch over their flocks at night. An angel of the Lord appeared to them, and the glory of the Lord shone around them, and they were terrified. But the angel said to them, "Do not be afraid. I bring you good news that will cause great joy for all the people. Today in the town of David a Savior has been born to you; he is the Messiah, the Lord. This will be a sign to you: You will find a baby wrapped in cloths and lying in a manger."

Suddenly a great company of the heavenly host appeared with the angel, praising God and saying,

> *Glory to God in the highest heaven,*
> *and on earth peace to those on whom his favor rests.*

When the angels had left them and gone into heaven, the shepherds said to one another, "Let's go to Bethlehem and see this thing that has happened, which the Lord has told us about."

Good news of great joy was coming to the whole world, but the announcement came only to one isolated group, and not a particularly religious one at that.

The responsibility of caring for their sheep made it difficult for shepherds to attend Temple or participate in the required Jewish festivals. They couldn't even observe the Sabbath properly by ceasing from work because their sheep needed to be taken care of every day.

It is not surprising these shepherds were terrified when the night sky began to glow brightly and an angel appeared to them; they could hardly expect good news to be given to people like themselves who looked bad and smelled worse.

Hearing the angel's message changed everything. Those who had always been outsiders and outcasts now went to check out the good news they had heard. We don't know what happened to the shepherds later, but we know they became part of God's story as it has been told every Christmas for 2,000 years.

The shepherds were a surprising choice to be the first to hear God's great news. If you were to invite some unsuspecting group into God's story today, who would you choose? What would you say?

MATTHEW 2:1-2,10-11

After Jesus was born in Bethlehem in Judea, during the time of King Herod, Magi from the east came to Jerusalem and asked, "Where is the one who has been born king of the Jews? We saw his star when it rose and have come to worship him."

When they saw the star, they were overjoyed. On coming to the house, they saw the child with his mother Mary, and they bowed down and worshiped him. Then they opened their treasures and presented him with gifts of gold, frankincense and myrrh.

The only thing more amazing than lowly shepherds being invited to celebrate the birth of the Christ Child was the invitation extended to the Magi.

These "wise men" were certainly not lowly as evidenced by their extravagant gifts fit for a king. The Magi were Zoroastrian astrologers from Persia (Iran on today's maps), adherents of a religion widely criticized by Jews in Jesus' day and Christians in our own. Yet these were the only people who grasped the significance of the natal star. God's people didn't know what God was doing; these outsiders did.

> *Have you ever had a significant conversation with someone from a different religion? Did it turn into an argument about who's right and who's wrong? Do you think there is a place for "Magi" in God's story today?*

MATTHEW 1:2-6

Abraham was the father of Isaac,
    Isaac the father of Jacob,
    Jacob the father of Judah and his brothers,
    Judah the father of Perez and Zerah,
       whose mother was Tamar,
    Perez the father of Hezron,
    Hezron the father of Ram,
    Ram the father of Amminadab,
    Amminadab the father of Nahshon,
    Nahshon the father of Salmon,
    Salmon the father of Boaz,
       whose mother was Rahab,
    Boaz the father of Obed,
       whose mother was Ruth,
    Obed the father of Jesse,
    and Jesse the father of King David.
David was the father of Solomon,
       whose mother had been Uriah's wife

Little is known about many of the men in the genealogy of Jesus, but the stories of the women listed in it are fascinating.

- ***Tamar*** *pretended to be a prostitute in order to become pregnant by her father-in-law (Genesis 38).*

- *Rahab* was a prostitute who saved her life by committing treason against her government (Joshua 2).

- *Ruth* was a Moabite woman, from a people whom God had forbidden to ever step on holy ground (Deuteronomy 23:3; Ruth 1-4).

- *Bathsheba* was either an adulteress or a rape victim whose pregnancy by King David brought about the murder of her husband (2 Samuel 11).

The cast of characters in God's story is truly remarkable in its diversity. Never assume that anyone you meet would be "the kind of person" who had no interest in hearing the good news of God's love revealed in Jesus.

> *Do you believe people with sordid pasts have a place in God's story? How would you go about inviting someone like this to discover new life in Christ?*

FOR REFLECTION AND DISCUSSION

To the extent you are comfortable doing so, share with your group your responses to the above questions.

PRAYER

Help me remember, Lord, that your story has more sinners than saints in it. Open my eyes to see those you are drawing to yourself, and show me how to invite them into your story.

5.2 INVITING INTO GOD'S PARTY

I once heard James Forbes, the pastor of New York's Riverside Church, speak at Northern Seminary. I don't remember which passage of Scripture was the basis for his sermon because he mentioned several around one central theme: God's Party.

What I most remember were the questions he asked: "How many of your churches are known for the parties you give? Would anyone confuse your worship service with a party?" We all had to admit that our churches were known for many things, but a "party atmosphere" was **not** one of them.

What is often called "The Parable of the Prodigal Son" is one of these stories about God's party. The repentance of the younger son and the recalcitrance of the older one must both be seen in the context of the extravagance of the father's love and the party he gave. Here is how Jesus tells the story:

LUKE 15:11-20

There was a man who had two sons. The younger one said to his father, "Father, give me my share of the estate." So he divided his property between them.

Not long after that, the younger son got together all he had, set off for a distant country and there squandered his wealth in wild living. After he had spent everything, there was a severe famine in that whole country, and he began to be in need. So he went and hired himself out to a citizen of that country, who sent him to his fields to feed pigs. He longed to fill his stomach with the pods that the pigs were eating, but no one gave him anything.

When he came to his senses, he said, "How many of my father's hired servants have food to spare, and here I am starving to death! I will set out and go back to my father and say to him: 'Father, I have sinned against heaven and against you. I am no longer worthy to be called your son; make me like one of your hired servants'." So he got up and went to his father.

But while he was still a long way off, his father saw him and was filled with compassion for him; he ran to his son, threw his arms around him and kissed him.

The Prodigal Son had broken his father's heart, first by desiring his father's money more than his father's love, then by going to a far country to escape his father's influence, and finally by squandering all he had been given of his father's wealth.

The young man's rebellion let him live "high on the hog" for a while, but ultimately he ended up living in the worst conditions imaginable. Eventually he "came to his senses" and realized the lowliest of his father's slaves had it better than he did.

Most earthly fathers would have hardened their hearts when treated so badly by a child, but Jesus told this story to show the depth of the Heavenly Father's love. Though having been disrespected and disregarded, the father persisted in looking for his son. When the son returned, the father was ready – not to scold him or make him the object of his wrath – but to welcome him back with open arms. The story continues:

How would you recognize today those who are broken, hopeless and far from God? Could you welcome them with open arms and share this story of God's love with them?

LUKE 15:21-32

The son said to him, "Father, I have sinned against heaven and against you. I am no longer worthy to be called your son."

But the father said to his servants, "Quick! Bring the best robe and put it on him. Put a ring on his finger and sandals on his feet. Bring the fattened calf and kill it. Let's have a feast and celebrate. For this son of mine was dead and is alive again; he was lost and is found." So they began to celebrate.

Meanwhile, the older son was in the field. When he came near the house, he heard music and dancing. So he called one of the servants and asked him what was going on. "Your brother has come," he replied, "and your father has killed the fattened calf because he has him back safe and sound."

The older brother became angry and refused to go in. So his father went out and pleaded with him. But he answered his father, "Look! All these years I've been slaving for you and never disobeyed your orders. Yet you never gave me even a young goat so I could celebrate with my friends. But when this son of yours who has squandered your property with prostitutes comes home, you kill the fattened calf for him!"

"My son," the father said, "you are always with me, and everything I have is yours. But we had to celebrate and be glad, because this brother of yours was dead and is alive again; he was lost and is found."

The father's delight at the prodigal's return stands in sharp contrast to the older son's disgust. The older son's obedience had been grudgingly carried out, leading him to think of himself as nothing more than an obedient slave with no evidence of either joy or gratitude in his life. At the death of his father he would become rich, but from his perspective his was a life of poverty.

In spite of all this, the father's love was shown to the older son. He left the party to entreat his older son to join in the celebration, reassuring him he didn't have to wait to begin to enjoy the life and inheritance that were already his.

From our perspective the story ends prematurely. What ending would you write for it? Would the older son join the party? Would he ever reconcile with the younger son?

The older son sounds remarkably like the Pharisees and scribes who were outraged that Jesus would embrace the prodigals, prostitutes, tax collectors and lepers of their day. How many church people today might identify with the older son? How would you go about inviting them to God's party?

FOR REFLECTION AND DISCUSSION

To the extent you are comfortable doing so, share with your group your responses to the above questions.

PRAYER

Open my eyes, Lord, to see those close at hand and those far away who are being drawn to you. Help me to join your party in celebration of your kingdom as it breaks into our world even now and as I look forward to its ultimate fulfillment with eager expectation.

5.3 INVITING INTO GOD'S FAMILY

The merger my church went through in 2010 had a lot to do with grandparents. We had been renting office space to a young church that had begun as a group of single "twenty-somethings" spun off from a nearby megachurch. It was not long before marriage and children entered the picture and the new church became what so many churches long to be: a spiritual home for young families.

This church, though, was interested in something different as became obvious when one of the pastors visited our office and saw a bulletin insert titled "Heritage Sunday." He asked about the stories of individuals being honored for membership in the church for 50, 60, 70 or 75 years.

"Do you really have people who've been part of your church for that long?" he asked. I explained this was only a portion of them because we were only recognizing the ones who had reached the various anniversaries during that year.

The pastor was not only amazed, but shared his longing to have the young families of his church connect with those in our church who were elders (not so much by office as by longevity). He went on to say that few of the many children in their church had any regular contact with grandparents or great-grandparents.

Not only was this one of the original factors that drew the two churches together, but it was also the beginning of redefining what we meant by "family." For many people this term connotes a father, a mother and their children living in a household. Such an understanding may have been broadly descriptive of life in the 1950s, but in the 2010 census only 20% of households fit that definition. That means 80% of households are excluded from what we typically think of as family.

Fortunately, the Bible has multiple images of what it means to be a family. Some of the Old Testament examples of families are controversial because they included slaves and multiple wives. The New Testament model of families that extends beyond blood and marriage ties, however, speaks powerfully to our context.

MARK 3:31-35

Then Jesus' mother and brothers arrived. Standing outside, they sent someone in to call him. A crowd was sitting around him, and they told him, "Your mother and brothers are outside looking for you."

"Who are my mother and my brothers?" he asked.

Then he looked at those seated in a circle around him and said, "Here are my mother and my brothers! Whoever does God's will is my brother and sister and mother."

We naturally think of families as having special privileges and responsibilities, but life in God's kingdom is different. Loving our neighbors as we love ourselves suggests we should **not** make sharp distinctions between the love we have for our families and the love we have for others. Members of our families are special, but no more so than everyone else.

The closest relationship we can have is not based on biology or proximity, but on shared values and perspectives. There is no one closer to us than those who seek to love and serve God as we do.

> *Do you know someone who is separated physically or emotionally from family? What would it look like for you to welcome that person into your family? What would be the first step?*

ACTS 2:40-47

With many other words he warned them; and he pleaded with them, "Save yourselves from this corrupt generation." Those who accepted his message were baptized, and about three thousand were added to their number that day.

They devoted themselves to the apostles' teaching and to fellowship, to the breaking of bread and to prayer. Everyone was filled with awe at the many wonders and signs performed by the apostles. All the believers were together and had everything in common. They sold property and possessions to give to anyone who had need. Every day they continued to meet together in the temple courts. They broke bread in their homes and ate together with glad and sincere hearts, praising God and enjoying the favor of all the people. And the Lord added to their number daily those who were being saved.

The early church practiced "life together" as seen in this story. With three thousand recent converts, it is likely they met in many homes rather than one large group. What is important to note, though, is that they prayed together, worshipped together, ate together and marveled at God's miracles together. No one imagined new believers might simply make a decision to accept Jesus and then go back to the life they had always known.

It is also important to note that life together meant sharing the good and the bad. Those who had financial resources helped out those who had none. This was not some form of primitive communism forced upon them by the government or even by religious leaders. It was just an example of what often happens when someone begins to take seriously what it means to "love your neighbor as yourself."

> *Have you experienced the kind of "life together" envisioned in this passage? If you were to start something like this, what would be the first step to take? Who would you invite?*

ACTS 10:23-33

The next day Peter started out with them, and some of the believers from Joppa went along. The following day he arrived in Caesarea. Cornelius was expecting them and had called together his relatives and close friends. As Peter entered the house, Cornelius met him and fell at his feet in reverence. But Peter made him get up. "Stand up," he said, "I am only a man myself."

While talking with him, Peter went inside and found a large gathering of people. He said to them: "You are well aware that it is against our law for a Jew to associate with or visit a Gentile. But God has shown me that I should not call anyone impure or unclean. So when I was sent for, I came without raising any objection. May I ask why you sent for me?"

Cornelius answered: "Three days ago I was in my house praying at this hour, at three in the afternoon. Suddenly a man in shining clothes stood before me and said, 'Cornelius, God has heard your prayer and remembered your gifts to the poor. Send to Joppa for Simon who is called Peter. He is a guest in the home of Simon the tanner, who lives by the sea.' So I sent for you immediately, and it was good of you to come. Now we are all here in the presence of God to listen to everything the Lord has commanded you to tell us."

It is hard to say who was more surprised by Peter's visit to the home of Cornelius. Peter was a devout Jew who could never imagine he would be the guest of a Gentile; Cornelius was someone who admired the Jews and their God, but never imagined he could show hospitality to one.

God's family is one that recognizes no barriers. We not only have the *freedom* to associate with people of backgrounds very different from our own; we have the *responsibility* to do so.

> *When was the last time you visited in the home of someone whose background was dramatically different from your own?*
>
> *When was the last time you invited into your home someone whose background was dramatically different from your own?*

FOR REFLECTION AND DISCUSSION

To the extent you are comfortable doing so, share with your group your responses to the above questions and the following:

How many are in your current family? Do you have room for more? Who comes to mind as someone you might invite to join you?

PRAYER

Thank you, Lord, for the family you have already given me and for the new family on the horizon. May we discover what it means to share life together, and may you be honored as we do so.

5.4 Inviting into God's Mission

Ken Follett in "Winter of the World" tells the story of Daisy, an American who traveled to England in the 1930s in search of something missing in her life. Though fabulously wealthy, she had been excluded from American high society because her family wealth was new and of questionable origin.

As a wealthy American heiress, Daisy set out to find the man who would give her the social status she desperately wanted. She married a member of the nobility and her entire life became a whirlwind of social events. She had no time or interest in anyone who was unable to advance her social standing.

World War II came and everything changed for Daisy when in the midst of a terrifying air raid she was pressed into service as an ambulance driver to take an injured child to the hospital. Although repulsed by the suffering she saw, Daisy found her efforts on behalf of those who were injured and dying brought meaning and purpose to her life.

There is nothing overtly religious about Daisy's story as Follett tells it, and yet it is a profound parable of entering into God's mission. Daisy had neither skill nor ability to rescue anyone, and yet she played a critical role by taking people to the one place where they could be helped.

The Bible describes much the same thing, but in the imagery of sheep and shepherds rather than bombing victims and hospitals. Jesus is the Good Shepherd who loves and cares for the lost sheep we find and bring to him. We invite others to join us in this mission; sometimes we even press people like Daisy into serving because the need is so great.

PSALM 23:1-6

The Lord is my shepherd, I shall not want.
  He makes me lie down in green pastures;
    he leads me beside still waters;
    he restores my soul.
He leads me in right paths
  for his name's sake.
Even though I walk through the darkest valley,
  I fear no evil; for you are with me;
  your rod and your staff— they comfort me.
You prepare a table before me
  in the presence of my enemies;
    you anoint my head with oil;
    my cup overflows.
Surely goodness and mercy shall follow me
  all the days of my life,
and I shall dwell in the house of the Lord
  my whole life long.

Psalm 23 speaks beautifully of green pastures and still waters, and of a shepherd's rod and staff to protect his sheep from danger. When they are with the shepherd, sheep have everything they need; apart from him, they are lost and vulnerable.

> *God has spoken to people through this Psalm in countless ways. What is God saying to you through it?*

115

MATTHEW 9:35-38

Jesus went through all the towns and villages, teaching in their synagogues, proclaiming the good news of the kingdom and healing every disease and sickness. When he saw the crowds, he had compassion on them, because they were harassed and helpless, like sheep without a shepherd. Then he said to his disciples, "The harvest is plentiful but the workers are few. Ask the Lord of the harvest, therefore, to send out workers into his harvest field."

Jesus mixed metaphors here, going from shepherds and sheep to harvests and workers, but the meaning is clear: we are to enter into God's mission and pray that others will enter into it with us.

What would it look like for you to bring harassed and helpless people to Jesus where they could find safety and wholeness? Who could you invite to join you in this mission?

LUKE 15:3-7

Then Jesus told them this parable: "Suppose one of you has a hundred sheep and loses one of them. Doesn't he leave the ninety-nine in the open country and go after the lost sheep until he finds it? And when he finds it, he joyfully puts it on his shoulders and goes home. Then he calls his friends and neighbors together and says, 'Rejoice with me; I have found my lost sheep.' I tell you that in the same way there will be more rejoicing in heaven over one sinner who repents than over ninety-nine righteous persons who do not need to repent.

Jesus told this parable to show that no one is expendable. There are no "acceptable losses" in God's mission because every person is of infinite value.

This parable shares a theme with the parables following it that speak of a lost coin and two lost sons (the prodigal and his older brother). In every case when the lost was found, there was rejoicing in heaven.

Where would you go today to find the harassed and helpless, lost and broken, neglected, overlooked and vulnerable?

Would you look only among the poor or would you be as likely to find such people among the middle class and rich?

What would be your first step after finding them?

FOR REFLECTION AND DISCUSSION

To the extent you are comfortable doing so, share with your group your responses to the above questions and the following:

If your group is continuing with your service project (or identifying a new one), who could you invite to join you from those you've connected with in the last few weeks?

PRAYER

Fill my heart with compassion, Lord, for those who are harassed and helpless in our own day. Show me who you are calling to join me in carrying out your mission, and give me boldness in inviting them.

MINISTRY REFLECTIONS

The following questions based on the lessons in this section can be discussed at each week's meeting or in a separate session.

1. *Did you have an opportunity to share with someone a part of God's story of the redemption and healing of the world? Did you invite them to become a part of God's answer rather than just a part of the world's problem?*

2. *Did you have an opportunity to meet some "prodigal sons" whose life choices have separated them from God's love and left them in life's pig pen? Did you have an opportunity to meet some "older brothers" whose pride and self-righteousness were revealed in disdain for those less fortunate? What did you do to invite into God's party any of those you met?*

3. *Have you begun to experience "life together" with people beyond your immediate family? Have you found someone to invite into your life and home? Have you accepted an invitation to enter into someone else's life and home?*

4. *Do you have a clear sense of how to find those who are lost in today's world? Have you invited someone to join you in looking for them and bringing them to Jesus?*

Resources, examples and stories about inviting people into *God's Story, God's Party, God's Family* and *God's Mission* are available on our website.

www.learningtoloveyourneighbor.com

STEP SIX:
CHALLENGING

For too much of my adult life I have been an undisciplined disciple. This is not to say I haven't believed in spiritual discipline. I've believed in it; I just haven't done it.

I don't think I've understood it very well either. Early in my Christian walk, I was told how important it was to have a daily quiet time in which I would read and memorize scripture. I should also spend much time in prayer in order to confess my sins and intercede on behalf of those in need. Keeping a journal also came highly recommended and worshipping in church every week was assumed.

When I added witnessing and serving to the above items, following Jesus began to feel like a full-time job.

What I should emphasize here is not so much the way it felt like a *full-time* job, but simply that it felt like a *job*. I tried hard to do what people were telling me to do, but I wasn't finding much life or joy in it.

I think this was partly due to being an extrovert who is energized more by spending time interacting with others than in being alone. In this sense it was good for me to end up in ministry because it drove me to the scriptures and prayer; I had to learn in order to teach.

A major turning point in my spiritual life happened more than thirty years ago when I went through a divorce. I remember clearly the sermon I gave to tell my congregation about it. The text was Mark 4:35-40.

That day when evening came, he said to his disciples, "Let us go over to the other side." Leaving the crowd behind, they took him along, just as he was, in the boat. There were also other boats with him. A furious squall came up, and the waves broke over the boat, so that it was nearly swamped. Jesus was in the stern, sleeping on a cushion. The disciples woke him and said to him, "Teacher, don't you care if we drown?"

He got up, rebuked the wind and said to the waves, "Quiet! Be still!" Then the wind died down and it was completely calm.

He said to his disciples, "Why are you so afraid? Do you still have no faith?"

I felt like the disciples in that storm: angry, hurt and afraid. They were following Jesus and about to drown while Jesus was sleeping in the back of the boat. Like them I cried out in anguish, "Don't you care?"

I ended the sermon by noting how the storm was calmed and the disciples were rescued, not because of their faith, but in spite of their lack of it. I knew there was no one but God who could calm the storm that was raging in my life and threatening to destroy me.

Reactions to the sermon surprised me because I hadn't polished it nearly as much as I usually did and I didn't think it was very well put together. People said it touched their hearts, though, because they knew it came from my heart. I began to see the huge difference between sermons based on what I knew God was saying to me versus what I thought God wanted to say to my congregation.

My life and ministry changed that morning as I began to learn that nothing was more important than allowing God to speak into my life in deep and powerful ways.

This focus has become clearer in recent years thanks to John Piippo, a friend since seminary. For more than 20 years John has led a presence-driven church whose corporate life and the lives of its members are centered on four elements of discipleship:

1. *Abide in Christ.*

2. *Saturate in Scripture.*

3. *Listen to what God says.*

4. *Obey what God says to do.*

These key elements of discipleship challenge me as I follow Jesus. They also provide a natural way for me to challenge others to do the same. I've organized this section of "Learning to Love Your Neighbor" around these four themes because they are the best and simplest understanding of discipleship I've found.[3]

As you abide, saturate, listen and obey, I am confident you will find yourself beginning to love God with all your heart and soul and mind and strength, and your neighbor as yourself. When that happens, you will know you have found your place in God's plan to fix a broken world.

---

[3] For more about John Piippo's ministry at Redeemer Community Church in Monroe, MI, check out his website: www.johnpiippo.com

6.1 CHALLENGING TO ABIDE

"Where do you live?" is a simple enough question that might bring forth answers like:

- I live in Michigan.
- I live in a red house on Hillside Drive.
- I live in a recliner in front of my television.

Suppose "Where do you live?" was asked in a deeper sense. The answers might be quite different:

- I live in a state of angry outbursts and apologies.
- I live in a roller coaster of highs and lows.
- I live in a flood of negative thoughts I can't escape.

As Jesus approached his death, he invited and challenged his disciples to live in a unique place: in him!

JOHN 15:4-5 (NRSV)

Abide in me as I abide in you. Just as the branch cannot bear fruit by itself unless it abides in the vine, neither can you unless you abide in me. I am the vine, you are the branches. Those who abide in me and I in them bear much fruit, because apart from me you can do nothing.

JOHN 15:9-11 (NRSV)

As the Father has loved me, so I have loved you; abide in my love. If you keep my commandments, you will abide in my love, just as I have kept my Father's commandments and abide in his love. I have said these things to you so that my joy may be in you, and that your joy may be complete.

JOHN 14:27

Peace I leave with you; my peace I give you. I do not give to you as the world gives. Do not let your hearts be troubled and do not be afraid.

"Abide" is used eight times in these short passages. Other translations have Jesus saying "live" in me or "remain" in me or "dwell" in me. All of these point to the same intimate, life-giving connection.

Jesus says if we don't live in him, we can do nothing. Of course, we actually ***can do a lot*** apart from Jesus, but if it's done out of pride or selfish ambition or to impress someone with how good we are, ***it just amounts to nothing***.

The Apostle Paul listed in Galatians the fruit we produce as we live in Christ versus living apart from him. This latter state is referred to by Paul as living "in the flesh."

GALATIANS 5:19-23

The acts of the flesh are obvious: sexual immorality, impurity and debauchery; idolatry and witchcraft; hatred, discord, jealousy, fits of rage, selfish ambition, dissensions, factions and envy; drunkenness, orgies, and the like. I warn you, as I did before, that those who live like this will not inherit the kingdom of God.

But the fruit of the Spirit is love, joy, peace, forbearance, kindness, goodness, faithfulness, gentleness and self-control.

The fruit of the Spirit listed here are not goals for which we strive or ideals by which we live; they are character traits of Jesus that come into us and flow out of us as we live in him and he lives in us. This is what Jesus told his disciples in the last hours he was with them before his death. Though the end of his life came soon, it wasn't the end of his relationship with those who followed him.

John Piippo says abiding in Christ means following the final instructions Jesus gave his disciples in John 14-16 with the result that:

- *I will experience his love*

- *I will experience his peace (not "peace" like our world gives)*

- *I will experience his joy*

- *With Christ in me I do the things that Jesus did*

- *I will not go up and down according to the circumstances of life*

- *I will not be a conference-dependent follower of Jesus*

- *I am a branch, connected to Jesus the True Vine*

- *My life will be fruit-bearing*

- *I will live in expectation. Today, and this week, could contain a watershed moment. Anything good and amazing can happen to the Jesus-follower who lives attached to Jesus, who lives "in Christ."*

What would it look like for you to abide in Jesus' love or live in his joy or rest in his peace?

In order to abide in Christ, are there things in your life you might need to start doing or stop doing?

FOR REFLECTION AND DISCUSSION

To the extent you are comfortable doing so, share with your group your responses to the above questions.

PRAYER

Blessed are you, O Lord our God, King of the Universe, who invites us and challenges us to abide in your love and in your joy and in your peace.

6.2 Challenging to Saturate

The Bible has been described as the world's least-read best-seller. Many people have excellent intentions when it comes to reading the Bible, but give up when they discover how confusing and difficult it can be.

In 2008 I wrote *Understanding the Old Testament: A Narrative Summary.* Many said they appreciated my doing this to help them understand the Old Testament. I told them that wasn't why I wrote it; I did it to help *me* understand the Old Testament.

I've come to realize I will never master the Bible. That's okay as long as I allow it to master me.

I'm not impressed when I hear pastors or teachers string together a multitude of Bible passages; such messages are often a mile wide and an inch deep. After listening to them, I don't say, "Wow! That speaker sure knows a lot of Scripture." I'm much more likely to think, "That speaker doesn't seem to know much about any Scripture."

It is nothing new for people to study the Bible diligently and still not get it. Jesus pointed out the same problem in his day when talking to some devout, religious people.

John 5:37-40 (NRSV)

And the Father who sent me has himself testified on my behalf. You have never heard his voice or seen his form, and you do not have his word abiding in you, because you do not believe him whom he has sent.

You search the scriptures because you think that in them you have eternal life; and it is they that testify on my behalf. Yet you refuse to come to me to have life.

Jesus was talking to people who were scrupulously religious and devoted students of the Hebrew Scriptures. They studied diligently and yet they failed to grasp the most important elements of the Scriptures because their minds were closed.

LUKE 24:44-45

He said to them, "This is what I told you while I was still with you: Everything must be fulfilled that is written about me in the Law of Moses, the Prophets and the Psalms."

Then he opened their minds so they could understand the Scriptures.

The Bible is both inspired and inspiring; the same Spirit involved in its writing is likewise involved in its reading. The key is to read it in a manner that allows God to speak to you through it.

Read-through-the-Bible-in-a-Year plans don't work very well for me. I've read the Bible several times that way, but my focus each day too often becomes getting through what I'm reading instead of letting what I'm reading get through to me.

One of the truly wonderful things about the Bible is this: you can go as deep in it as you want and never touch bottom. There are passages from which I've preached time and again only to discover God saying something completely new to me the next time I read it.

JOHN 15:7-8 (NRSV)

If you abide in me, and my words abide in you, ask for whatever you wish, and it will be done for you. My Father is glorified by this, that you bear much fruit and become my disciples.

Abiding in Jesus and being saturated in Scripture are keys to a fruitful life. John Piippo says it means this for him:

- *I will take the Book and read*

- *I will meditate on the biblical text*

- *I will slow-cook in the teriyaki sauce of God's thoughts and God's ways and God's promises*

- *I will shut my ears to our hyper-wordy world and attend to the deep words of Scripture*

- *I will fix my eyes, not on things seen, but on things unseen*

- *I will be illuminated by God's Spirit*

- *God's Spirit will escort my heart to its true home*

What is your pattern for Scripture reading? Do you sense the words of Jesus living in you as you live in him?

What barriers or obstacles do you face as you attempt to saturate your life in Scripture?

FOR REFLECTION AND DISCUSSION

To the extent you are comfortable doing so, share with your group your responses to the above questions.

PRAYER

Thank you, Jesus, for coming to us full of grace and truth. May your words abide in us as we abide in you, and may our lives bear much fruit as we do this.

6.3 Challenging to Listen

In 2002 I considered myself extremely fortunate to be the pastor of Moraine Valley Community Church. I had served there for six years and had seen God bring new life in ways beyond anything I could have imagined. I was 55 years old and assumed I would stay at the church until I retired.

God had other plans. One day as I was walking around admiring the new landscaping, God whispered to me, "You are not to stay here to watch this grow."

I was dumbfounded. I sensed this was the quiet voice of God I had come to know over the years, but this time it just didn't make sense. This was a wonderful church and God was obviously using me to make a difference in people's lives. Why would God send me to another church where I would have to start all over?

I didn't say anything to anyone for a few days, but the message had the kind of quiet persistence so typical of God. Finally I worked up the courage to tell my wife. I was sure she would say I must be crazy, but she surprised me even more by saying, "I've been wondering if God might call you someplace else."

It was the last thing I expected her to say, and it was clear confirmation that this was indeed a message from God.

Over the years I have come to recognize God speaking to me. On a few occasions it has been loud and insistent, but only when I have allowed myself to become distracted by other things to the point I was paying little attention to God.

One of the clear ways God speaks to me is through the Bible. I regularly find a particular word or verse standing out to me as I read a familiar text. Sometimes I am struck by a phrase I've never noticed before. What grabs my attention is not necessarily the most important part of the text; it's just something God wants me to look at right then.

Another way God speaks to me is through a short phrase or idea that pops into my head. I know of no way to explain it other than saying there is for me a clear difference between what I'm thinking on my own and what comes to me from elsewhere.

I make it a practice to tell others what I'm hearing from God because I believe to do so is both a privilege and a responsibility of living in community. It keeps my feet on solid ground.

JOHN 10:2-5

The one who enters by the gate is the shepherd of the sheep. The gatekeeper opens the gate for him, and the sheep listen to his voice. He calls his own sheep by name and leads them out. When he has brought out all his own, he goes on ahead of them, and his sheep follow him because they know his voice. But they will never follow a stranger; in fact, they will run away from him because they do not recognize a stranger's voice."

Having grown up on a farm, I'm familiar with this idea of animals recognizing the voice of the one who feeds and cares for them.

Imagine how wonderful it would be to have a church with members who individually and collectively were so familiar with God's voice they would have a clear sense of where God was leading them.

John Piippo describes listening to what God says in this way:

- *I will be alert*
- *I will live with ears wide open*
- *God has much to say to me this week*
- *Today, I have "ears to hear"*
- *When God speaks to me, I will write it down in my journal*
- *I will remember the words of the Lord to me*
- *God will tell me that he loves me*
- *God will shepherd me*
- *God will lead me in paths of righteousness, not for my glory, but for his sake*

How clearly do you recognize God's voice speaking directly to you or speaking to you through Scripture?

What "noise" in your life might act as a barrier when it comes to listening for God's "still, small voice?"

FOR REFLECTION AND DISCUSSION

To the extent you are comfortable doing so, share with your group your responses to the above questions.

PRAYER

Quiet me down, Lord, so I can hear your voice and not be left to find my own path through the unknown future that lies before me.

6.4 CHALLENGING TO OBEY

My wife and I have long believed in what we call "God's will for dummies." What that means to us is when God's call is clear, it's time to move!

Our call to Moraine Valley Community Church had been like that. As described earlier, our call to leave MVCC was equally clear. Based on what God had said to me about leaving, I sent out letters to some key contacts letting them know I was open to being called elsewhere. Then I waited to hear from someone.

Nothing happened for 18 months and I began to wonder if I had misunderstood what God was telling me. Then I heard from a church in Michigan and it soon became clear that this was the church to which God was calling me.

The First Baptist Church of Royal Oak had a marvelous heritage, but had also been in steady decline for nearly 40 years. I assumed God was calling me there to bring the same kind of miraculous growth and renewal I had seen at MVCC.

I was wrong. In the first three years I conducted 35 funerals, and all our young families left because they wanted a church with more for their children. When the dust settled our annual giving had declined by $150,000.

As I look back on it now, our years in Royal Oak were perhaps the hardest and yet the best time of our lives. Hardly anything went as we expected and yet God's hand could be seen in everything. It wasn't a matter of a few hard years while I "learned my lesson;" God was leading me where I had never gone before. It ended up being wonderful, but nothing like I had imagined.

Obedience does not come easily for me. I was never in the military and perhaps that is a good thing. I probably would have obeyed my orders, but I almost certainly would have questioned them. I know I was never satisfied when my parents answered my questions with, "Because I said so."

I have learned it is different with God. If God had tried to explain why I was being called to Royal Oak, I don't think I could have understood. Only now does it all make sense.

JOHN 10:3-4

He calls his own sheep by name and leads them out. When he has brought out all his own, he goes on ahead of them, and his sheep follow him because they know his voice.

This is one of my favorite images of the church. It shows each person in a relationship with God who can call each one by name because he knows us so well. It also shows each person recognizes and follows the voice of God.

It would be a mistake, though, to imagine this text is speaking about our individual relationship with God. When sheep hear the shepherd's voice and follow where he leads, they inevitably end up going in the same direction. When sheep do whatever they want, however, they always end up wandering everywhere and getting lost.

This image leads to a clear and simple vision for every church: Following Jesus Together.

Is your community of faith united and following Jesus together or more like a ragtag collection of wandering sheep?

Step Six: Challenging

John Piippo has described obeying what God says to do like this:

- *God will direct my paths*

- *God will make my paths straight*

- *The inner "GPS" ("God Positioning System") is turned on*

- *Where he leads me, I will follow*

- *I will experience life as an adventure*

- *In obedience to God, my life finds meaning and purpose*

FOR REFLECTION AND DISCUSSION

To the extent you are comfortable doing so, share with your group your responses to the above questions.

PRAYER

Help me trust you, Lord, walking by faith wherever you lead me and trusting it will be where I need to go.

Ministry Reflections

The challenge of discipleship impacts how you live your life and how you minister to others in the context God has given you. The following questions based on the lessons in this section can be discussed at each week's meeting or in a separate session.

1. *Within your ministry context this past week, in what way have you been abiding in Jesus by dwelling in his love or living in his joy or resting in his peace?*

2. *Within your ministry context this past week, in what way has Scripture been your focus and how have you saturated your life in it?*

3. *Within your ministry context this past week, what has God been saying to you?*

4. *Within your ministry context this past week, what steps have you taken to obey what God has said to do?*

5. *During this past week, in what way has your involvement in a community of faith impacted your ministry context?*

Epilogue

Okay. So you've finished *Learning to Love Your Neighbor*. Here are some questions to review your experience:

1. **Did you do what you committed to do?**

    a. *Were you able to find time most days to be with God?*

    b. *Did you read this book with others and meet consistently to discuss it?*

    c. *Did you discover how your life is a ministry context providing opportunity to connect with new and old friends, family, neighbors, co-workers and others?*

    d. *Did your group find an opportunity to serve people outside the normal circles you travel?*

2. **Did God do something special in your life?**

    a. *Did you come to recognize God's voice more clearly and grasp what God was saying to you?*

    b. *Did God bring people into your life who surprised you by the extent to which God was already at work in them?*

    c. *Did the experience of ministering to others bring profound change into your own life?*

3. **Did you find your place in God's plan to fix a broken world?**

137

Regardless how you answered these questions, I encourage you to consider reading this book again, but not in the same way as before. One way to guarantee newness is to add one or two people to your group. Another way change comes is by making a new commitment to create more time and space in your life for God.

START A NEW GROUP

If God brought new people into your life or if you connected with old friends in new ways, you may well be ready to start and lead a new group. Ask God to show you who you should ask and then say something like this:

I just read a book I think you might really enjoy. It didn't involve much reading actually, but there was a lot to think about. Each week a few of us met to talk about it.

The whole experience was so positive I decided to read the book again with a different group. I've been thinking and praying about who I would want to invite and you were at the top of my list.

The book is called Learning to Love Your Neighbor: Finding Your Place in God's Plan to Fix a Broken World. If you think you might be interested, I'd be glad to give you a copy of the book to look at. We can talk more about it later.

As soon as you have two or three people who are interested you can figure out the best time and place to meet. Your group will probably work best if you have at least three people involved, and no more than eight.

If everyone who reads this book as part of a group gathers a new group to read it afterward, you can imagine the potential for growth. I believe this is the kind of multiplication Jesus was talking about when he gave the Great Commission to his disciples in Matthew 28:18-20:

Step Six: Challenging

Then Jesus came to them and said, "All authority in heaven and on earth has been given to me. Therefore go and make disciples of all nations, baptizing them in the name of the Father and of the Son and of the Holy Spirit, and teaching them to obey everything I have commanded you. And surely I am with you always, to the very end of the age."

May you live to see the Great Commission fulfilled as you learn to love your neighbor and as you find your place in God's plan to fix a broken world!

For information on bulk purchases of 5 copies or more for small group use, go to the website:

www.learningtoloveyourneighbor.com

LEADING A GROUP

Those who lead small groups are facilitators, not teachers. Your role is not to get people to the point where you think they should be, but to create a safe environment in which people can be honest and open and in which God can move in a process of transformation.

The focus the first week will be to let people get comfortable with each other. Explain that anyone can decline at any point to do anything asked; no one will be pushed to pray or share if not willing to do so. It is also important to establish confidentiality; what is said in the group stays in the group unless permission is given to share it outside.

Each week's meeting should not be longer than an hour unless the group agrees more time is needed. The format goes something like this:

GATHERING TIME

Encourage people to be prompt, but realize most groups struggle to get everyone there at the same time. As people arrive, have them begin talking about how their week has gone. If needed to get people talking ask, "What were the high and low points of your week? Where did you see evidence of God's presence?"

As the weeks go by, expect this portion of the meeting to get longer as people share what God is doing in their life and ministry.

OPENING PRAYER

The first week you will want to pray unless you know another person in the group would be comfortable doing so. After the first week invite someone else to pray. It is often helpful to ask before the meeting begins in order to avoid embarrassing someone who is not yet comfortable praying in public.

There may often be times you will choose to pray as a group. Invite people to pray as they feel led to do so and appoint someone to close the prayer time unless you do it yourself.

DISCUSSION QUESTIONS

Each chapter will have a number of questions for reflection and discussion. Everyone should have opportunity to share with the group, but it is not necessary that every person answer every question. Some questions will resonate with people much more than others.

If a particular question generates minimal discussion, move on to the next question. If discussion becomes lengthy, you will need to decide whether to cut it off or let it continue. You may also choose to ask the group what it wants to do. There may be times when the group decides to spend an extra meeting on a particular set of questions. You will probably cover one chapter each week and one section each month. It is possible, however, you will go faster or slower. It is important to find a pace that works for you and your group, but recognize going too fast is more of a problem than going too slow.

CLOSING PRAYER

The closing prayer has much in common with the opening one except it focuses more on what happened in the meeting and what steps come next for individuals and for the group. You may want to pray together the prayer printed at the end of the week's material.

Further resources on leading a small group are available on the website:

www.learningtoloveyourneighbor.com

ACKNOWLEDGMENTS

In some ways this book began while I was part of a Together in Ministry Group sponsored by the Ministers' Council of the ABC-USA. Under the leadership of Rev. Dr. Daniel Buttry, a number of clergy gathered to support each other even as we were stretched in our approach to ministry. It was here I first encountered the concept of the missional church.

Under the leadership of Rev. Dr. Roy Medley, the American Baptist Churches, USA, embarked on a "Transformed by the Spirit" initiative at the June 2011 Biennial in Puerto Rico. The heart of this initiative was the recognition our churches faced "adaptive challenges" for which we had no ready answers and no experts to guide us.

The American Baptist Churches of Michigan focused on two of these adaptive challenges: discipleship and evangelism. This book is in large measure a response to those challenges.

Two churches mentioned in this book have impacted me in powerful ways. Genesis in Royal Oak taught me much about what a church focused on discipleship and following Jesus together could be. Its pastors, Beau McCarthy, Drew Hunter and Nate Sjogren, are far more than friends or colleagues; each has affirmed and challenged me more than I could ever have imagined and yet they are the age of my children. How can that be?

It was also through Genesis I first heard of Mike Breen and 3DM. Mike's approach to discipleship resonated strongly with me.

Those familiar with the 3DM program will doubtless recognize the influence of their thinking at several points in this book.

Harbert Community Church is near the town where my wife and I retired in 2013. Even before we arrived, the church asked if I would become their interim pastor. I was delighted to do so, particularly when I realized I would have a three-month window to do a "90-Day 'Love Your Neighbor' Adventure" I had been working on for the American Baptist Transformed by the Spirit initiative. What God did in my life during those months became the basis for this book. The support and affirmation I've received at this Evangelical Covenant church has been nothing short of phenomenal.

The "90-Day Adventure" included a daily Bible study sent via email to about 200 people and nearly 50 pastors. As I started putting the book together, I invited these same people to serve as informal editors and 48 agreed to do so. Among those who gave feedback to me are: Bev Babb, Ron Gregg, Rev. Jay Fast, Doris Kallberg, Bob and Linda Miller, Sandi Morris, Margaret Nyman, Eileen Petersen, Anne Russell, Dorothy Simmons, Nancy Wenstrand, and my sister, Judy Day.

There were others within the group of 48 whose comments merit special mention: John Daniels, Sue Fabian, Jane Gunneman, Susan Knight, Ruby Rorabaugh and Mike Williams. These six gave far more (and better) feedback than I had any right to expect.

My daughter, Amanda Macarrau, took the cover photo and was very helpful in finalizing the cover design. Hailey Halsel took the photo on the back cover.

Last and most important is my wife, Linnea. She has shaped by life in countless ways during our many years of marriage and her commitment to love God and neighbor continues to challenge me. She is my best friend, my best editor and the best partner I could ever have in the adventure of following Jesus.

INDEX OF SCRIPTURES

Learning to Love Your Neighbor